FUNNY STUFF

THE
FUNNY STUFF

Also by P. J. O'Rourke

THE
FUNNY STUFF

THE OFFICIAL P. J. O'ROURKE
QUOTATIONARY AND RIFFAPEDIA

P. J. O'ROURKE

EDITED BY TERRY MCDONELL

WITH AN INTRODUCTION BY CHRISTOPHER BUCKLEY

Atlantic Monthly Press
New York

FIRST EDITION

Published simultaneously in Canada
Printed in the United States of America

First Grove Atlantic hardcover edition: November 2022

Library of Congress Cataloging-in-Publication data is available for this title.

ISBN 978-0-8021-6064-5
eISBN 978-0-8021-6065-2

Atlantic Monthly Press
an imprint of Grove Atlantic
154 West 14th Street
New York, NY 10011

Distributed by Publishers Group West

groveatlantic.com

22 23 24 25   10 9 8 7 6 5 4 3 2 1

For
Christina Mallon O'Rourke
Elizabeth Helena O'Rourke
Olivia Christine O'Rourke
Edward Clifford Kelly O'Rourke

CONTENTS

INTRODUCTION
CHRISTOPHER BUCKLEY

P. J. O'Rourke was the funniest American writer of his generation, as well as one of the smartest and most prolific. In the lonely months since he died, I've been asking myself: What made him so darn quotable? When some years ago Penguin published *The Dictionary of Modern Humorous Quotations*, he had more entries in it than any other living writer.

Now he has an entire book of quotations all to himself, edited by longtime friend Terry McDonell. Normally, I'd say what a "painstaking" job Terry did in creating this "monumental work," but all he had to do was pluck one low-hanging fruit after another. In fact, he probably rented a combine harvester from the literary division of John Deere. The hardest part must have been deciding what *not* to include. Now that he belongs to the ages, P. J. O'Rourke takes his rightful place along with Oscar Wilde, Mark Twain, and Dorothy Parker in the Pantheon of Quote Gods.

I never read or listened to P.J. without thinking, "Wish I'd said that." In an article for the *New York Times* after his death, I called him "hyperaphoristic." This annoyed many readers because they had to look it up. Whatever you call someone who dispenses aphorisms, bon mots, maxims, axioms, epigrams, and apothegms, P.J. was a conveyor belt of verbal pearls. I can hear him saying, "'Conveyor belt of verbal pearls?' Mixed metaphor alert!" Okay. Conveyor belt of apothegms. Happy now?

Some people are born witty, others achieve wit, and others have wit thrust upon them. Did Patrick Jake O'Rourke spring from his mother's womb and say to the physician who delivered him, "Doctor Livingstone, I presume?" Or "Get me out of this wet placenta and into a dry martini"?

His Buick-salesman father died when P.J. was nine. O'Rourke père used to take his son with him to bars. I see O'Rourke fils— French for "squirt"—sitting there, listening to the grown-up repartee and jokes. *We don't get many eight-year-olds in here. No, and at these prices, you aren't likely to.*

He was a proud son of Toledo, Ohio. This pedigree made him 100 percent red, white, and blue Americano. Ohio is famous for providing us with presidents, but it has also given us P.J., James Thurber, Donald Ogden Stewart, Erma Bombeck, Dave Chappelle, and Ambrose Bierce (also, Madalyn Murray O'Hair, who was funny in her own way). Could it be something in the water? Ohio water was famous at one point for actually being flammable. P.J. was determined to write the definitive history of Toledo "from the beginning of time to the end of the universe." He never did. The loss to history is immeasurable, but his Toledoness remained a quintessential part of him.

He went to Miami University, Ohio, which, as he pointed out, was not the University of Miami, where you could major in water skiing. He left the American heartland for the American littoral—specifically, Baltimore, where he got a master's degree in English lit at Johns Hopkins.

It struck me just now as I typed "Baltimore" that the city was the lifelong home of H. L. Mencken. P.J. probably had to read Joyce's *Ulysses* to get that master's degree. One of the key words in that cinder block of literature is "metempsychosis."

You remember metempsychosis. Oh, right, you had to look up "hyperaphoristic." It means the transmigration of a soul from one person into another. What I'm driving at in my pedantic and precious way is that P. J. O'Rourke was the H. L. Mencken of his day.

His first job in journalism was at a lefty underground rag called *Harry*. It folded after a mob occupied its offices to protest *Harry*'s insufficient Leninism. He migrated up the Acela corridor avant la lettre (look it up) to New York and a job at *National Lampoon* magazine. Toledo Kid meets Harvard Smart-Asses. Result: *serious* funniness.

In memory yet green is the moment the *National Lampoon 1964 High School Yearbook Parody* hit the newsstands. If you're an aging boomer like me who now pays attention to the continence-aids ads on the evening news, you remember that moment too. The yearbook was a game changer. A weather changer. An underwear changer, because you laughed so hard you had to change, even though you weren't incontinent then.

Masquerading as the yearbook of C. Estes Kefauver Memorial High School in Dacron, Ohio, this encyclopedic work of comic genius was largely a collaboration between Doug Kenney, a *Lampoon* cofounder, and its rising star staffer, P. J. O'Rourke. It has sold over two million copies. Kenney took the school motif to the next level by cowriting the script for *Animal House*.

So here's my big, never-until-now-revealed, groundbreaking theory—namely, that P.J.'s apprenticeship at the *Lampoon* was the launchpad of his hyperapho . . . his Quote-Dynamo. I'm prepared to go out on a limb no man has gone out on before and posit that it was at the *Lampoon* that P. J. O'Rourke found his voice. It was the strop on which he stropped the razor of his . . .

He left us twenty-one books, among them *Parliament of Whores* (about Washington, natch), *Eat the Rich, Give War a*

Chance, Peace Kills, How the Hell Did This Happen? (about the 2016 election, natch), and *Don't Vote—It Just Encourages the Bastards.* His final one was *A Cry from the Far Middle.*

The last time I was with him, he said, "I'm tired. I've been doing this for over half a @#$%ing century." He did not actually say "ampersandhashtagdollarsignpercent." He used a shorter word. He may have been tired—who wouldn't be after half a fucking century?—but it didn't show on the page. The Toledo Kid pitched fastballs up to the bottom of the ninth.

Those twenty-one books, sometimes misfiled in the "Humor" ghetto in bookstores, include a dissertation on Adam Smith's *The Wealth of Nations.* P.J. wasn't in it only for the funny. He was a Serious Man—his forebear Mencken would have said "an *ernst Mann*"—who didn't take himself seriously. Self-seriousness is a serious impediment to wit. It's not that he lacked ego. "Egoless writer" is a *very* funny oxymoron. He wore his credentials lightly because he saw himself as just another player in the Human Comedy.

Terry has done a great job of combine harvesting the O'Rourkean oeuvre—oo-ver, as P.J. would pronounce it. It must have been a fun labor of love. Reading P. J. O'Rourke is like spooning up caviar with a ladle. And being his friend for forty years was even better than driving fast on drugs while getting your wing-wang squeezed and not spilling a drop.

Wish I'd said that.

Editor's Note
Editing P.J.
Terry McDonell

Chris Buckley points out in his slyly quotable introduction that P. J. O'Rourke was the most quoted man on the planet and goes on to suggest that as the editor of this compendium I needed only to pluck one low-hanging fruit after another. Well, fair enough.

Two days after P.J. passed, Matt Labash, who got to know P.J. in Kuwait during the 2003 Iraq War, wrote in his *Slack Tide* newsletter that P.J. was such a good writer that he left "at least one chocolate on the pillow in every paragraph he wrote" and then proved it by randomly opening five of P.J.'s books and calling out the first passage he saw in each (all included in this volume). That's how good P.J. was—incapable of writing a flat paragraph.

The only editorial solution was to break the "only-one-liners" rule and select paragraphs as well, which means you can read this volume more or less in line with Labash's proof of P.J. as a Great Writer. Make that GREAT WRITER!—the kind of amplification P.J. would never use.

*   *   *

In 1970 P.J. lived in a triangle-shaped apartment above the Midtown Tunnel in Manhattan. The living room came to a point like the bow of a ship heading uptown on First Avenue. Other writers knew P.J. as the *National Lampoon* editor who had put a dog on the cover with a pistol in his ear and the headline: "If You Don't Buy This Magazine, We'll Kill This Dog." I'm not sure why, but that coverline and that pointed apartment seemed to match.

He told me that whenever he had a little money in the bank, he applied for higher credit lines and that I should too.

"It's not like we've got a secure future," he said. He had just gone freelance.

"Time to grow up," he said. "We're screwed."

Well, P.J. wasn't screwed because it was clear that he was going to figure out something smart for himself—maybe even as a writer. I wondered how high he had pushed his credit lines.

Many of his *Lampoon* colleagues were stepping easily into the movie business, starting with *Animal House* (1978). P.J. took his shot with a Rodney Dangerfield vehicle called *Easy Money* and used the payday as a down payment on a small house in New Hampshire and a Porsche. The problem was that he hated the work as much as he loved the 911 Turbo.

"It's just a stupid movie," P.J. said, as we were driving from New Hampshire to Boston. He was going to drop me off at the airport and then spend the day working with Rodney on the script.

"Come on . . . ," I said. Like everyone I knew in journalism, I was envious of movie money.

"I should know how bad it is," he said. "I'm writing it . . ."

Unlike Rodney, what was funny to P.J. was never loud or slapstick or absurd, and he loved language, which made editing him joyous—not a word often associated with the editorial process. He might occasionally drop an ironic straight line about deadlines being his friends, but he always met them on exact word count with clean copy. He was a tight grammarian, by which I mean his grammar was immaculate. The structural rules governing composition reflected his love of logic. He could talk about *morphology* ("the study of the forms of things"), a word he taught me. Copy editors loved him until they realized he was better at their jobs than they were.

Our first piece together was "Cocaine Etiquette," at *Rolling Stone.* P.J. wrote: "Cocaine and etiquette are inseparable, they go together like cocaine and, well, more cocaine." We were working from the inside out. Sometimes all we did was laugh, although actually *laughing* is something P.J. never did. I had just edited this:

Q. What should be served with cocaine?

A. Most people enjoy a couple thousand cigarettes with their "face Drano." Others mix "indoor Aspen Lift lines" with multiple sedatives that achieve that marvelous feeling so similar to not having taken drugs at all. But everyone, whether he wants to or not, should drink plenty of whiskey or gin. If you smell strongly of alcohol, people may think you are drunk instead of stupid.

The explosiveness came with the pop at the end—an obvious (logical) truth underlining the point he was making. It worked with his funny stuff and, more powerfully, when his irony turned hard. I'll point to a piece I did not edit—P.J. on Somalia:

Before the marines came, the children were dying like . . . "Dying like flies" is not a simile you'd use in Somalia.

The flies wax prosperous and lead full lives. Before the marines came, the children were dying like children.

That Somalia piece, "All Guns, No Butter," was for *Rolling Stone* after P.J. went on contract and was listed on the masthead as "The Foreign Affairs Desk." What he mostly did in that job was travel the world from war zone to war zone, filling his notebooks with concise if sometimes wrenching reporting that he ran through an IBM Selectric back home in New Hampshire or Washington, DC, where he had taken an apartment to be close to what was becoming his default target, Big Government. His first book about politics was *Parliament of Whores*, and you could see he was building on what he called his "Pants-Down Republican" conceit. "Giving money and power to government is like giving whiskey and car keys to teenage boys. . . ."

Beyond his one-liners, P.J.'s basic construct was to take familiar concepts like, say, God and Santa Claus, push them to their logical extreme with a coating of his seemingly good-natured biases, and end with a hilarious (and logical) kicker, as shown in this quote from his 1991 *Parliament of Whores*:

I have only one firm belief about the American political system, and that is this: God is a Republican and Santa Claus is a Democrat.

God is an elderly or, at any rate, middle-aged male, a stern fellow, patriarchal rather than paternal and a great believer in rules and regulations. He holds men accountable for their actions. He has little apparent concern for the material well-being of the disadvantaged. He is politically connected, socially powerful and holds the mortgage on literally everything in the world. God is difficult. God is unsentimental. It is very hard to get into God's heavenly country club.

Santa Claus is another matter. He's cute. He's non-threatening. He's always cheerful. And he loves animals. He may know who's been naughty and who's been nice, but he never does anything about it. He gives everyone everything they want without the thought of a quid pro quo. He works hard for charities, and he's famously generous to the poor. Santa Claus is preferable to God in every way but one: There is no such thing as Santa Claus.*

When he branched out from *Rolling Stone*, it was to the *Atlantic Monthly*, the *American Spectator*, the *Weekly Standard*, and the Cato Institute. You could see his interests shifting toward policy. The bestsellers had started when P.J. walked away from *Easy Money* and they kept coming. P.J. quotes got passed around like, well, P.J. quotes. For a while (before the internet), I kept a file of them, including some long paragraphs. I used short ones to spice my letters and sent long ones to writers as unsubtle suggestions to take some chances. I have included many of them here, and I have probably angered the Quotation Gods by also occasionally quoting myself above without attribution—something P.J. never did. Finally, in the interest of space, context, and clarity, I occasionally cherry-picked and/or shortened passages—something that is always dangerous to do with a great writer. But then, as P.J. liked to put it, *safety has no place anywhere.*

Some editing to P.J.'s riffs and quotes was done for clarity, continuity, and humor.

---

* P. J. O'Rourke, *Parliament of Whores: A Lone Humorist Attempts to Explain the Entire U. S. Government*, 1991.

THE
FUNNY STUFF

PART I

AMERICA
AND
AMERICANS

Consider someone who had never been to America. What would he or she think, after being Blockbustered, Safewayed, Chevroned, Shelled, Dodged, Nissaned, Wal-Marted, Dress Barned, Gapped, Levied, Burger Kinged, Dairy Queened, and Taco Belled? Would he have a good impression of the United States? No. Would he have an accurate impression? That's another matter.

—*The CEO of the Sofa* (2001)

We don't need a wall on our border; we need gates with turnstiles and ticket-takers. The right way to limit immigration (and make people in foreign countries pay for it) is to charge admission to the United States. Disneyland costs $100 a day. There are at least 12 million illegal immigrants in America. By my calculation, we're leaving $438 billion a year on the table.

—*How the Hell Did This Happen?* (2017)

AMERICA

America is the only nation in the world based on happiness. Read the Magna Charta, the Communist Manifesto, the Ten Commandments, the Analects of Confucius, Plato's Republic, the New Testament or the UN Charter, and find me any happiness at all. America is the Happy Kingdom.

—Parliament of Whores (1991)

The fat and stupid are a vital part of America.

—The CEO of the Sofa (2001)

AMERICANS

Americans are remarkably puritanical—when they aren't high as kites.

—The CEO of the Sofa (2001)

We Americans are an unprincipled nation. Not that we're bad or anything. It's just that it's hard for us to pay attention to abstract matters when we have so many concrete matters—cellular phones, ski boats, salad shooters, trail bikes, Stair-Masters, snowboards, pasta-making machines—to occupy us.

—Parliament of Whores (1991)

We've become a nation of immense nine-year-olds dressed for all occasions in T-shirts, shorts, and Tevas. Or, sometimes, just to change things up, pajama pants, sports bras, and wife-beater shirts.

—None of My Business (2018)

There are always groups of people upon whom to blame things. But there's no group of people upon whom to blame *every-thing*, except in a free and democratic society where we can, with confidence, blame everything on ourselves.

—Don't Vote—It Just Encourages the Bastards (2010)

ANGER

Maybe the answer to America's current state of angry per-plexity is "Everybody must get stoned." It's certainly an idea that's trending. But I was around the last time we tried that. And perhaps this is an historical period that we should re-examine.

—The CEO of the Sofa (2001)

ANIMAL RIGHTS

With all due respect to advocates for animal rights, what about animal responsibilities?

—A Cry from the Far Middle (2020)

BAILOUTS

We have the cow of economic freedom. Do we take the cow to market and trade her for the magic beans of bailout and stimulus? When we climb that beanstalk we're going to find a giant government at the top. Are we going to be as lucky as Jack the giant killer was? I'm not sure Jack himself was that lucky with his giant killing. My guess is that Jack spent years being investigated by giant subcommittees and now Jack's paying a giant tax on his beanstalk bonus.

—*Don't Vote—It Just Encourages the Bastards* (2010)

BANKS

Kill the spending. Fuck the regulations. Marry an investment banker.

—*Don't Vote—It Just Encourages the Bastards* (2010)

At a subconscious level we all have an image of banks as being like Scrooge McDuck's money vault. We put our money in banks, and bankers put that money—all those ones and fives and dimes and quarters—into a great big safe, where they rub it and dust it and stack it in piles, and where sometimes, late at night, the bankers take off all their clothes and roll in the stuff and yell, "Whee!"

—*None of My Business* (2018)

What I want is a compact household-size type of Central Bank for my own personal use. A small, handy "Central Bank of

O'Rourke" that would fit in the laundry room or in the mud-room between the dog kennels.

—*None of My Business* (2018)

BIG GOVERNMENT

Great, hulking, greasy, obese, gobbling, omnivorous, ever-aggrandizing, fat-witted government—I am not its friend. In Washington, the Republicans are (in their wing-tip-hobbled, suspender-entangled, Old Spice–befogged way) trying to destroy big government. The Republicans I like okay. The destruction I adore.

—*Age and Guile Beat Youth, Innocence, and a Bad Haircut* (1995)

BOARDING SCHOOLS

Rich children are shipped to boarding schools, often before they are weaned. A child who was kept in the Bronx Zoo for twelve years would acquire more courtesy and taste.

—*Modern Manners* (1983)

Occasionally boarding schools do turn out someone along the lines of the "preppy" stereotype. But in real life their graduates are more likely to wind up playing electronic xylophone, and singing fifties toothpaste commercials in a performance art ensemble.

—*Modern Manners* (1983)

THE BUSH FAMILY

Our families are big. The Bush family, for example, is so big that one presidency wasn't enough for them, let alone one SUV.

—*Driving Like Crazy* (2009)

Jeb should not have heeded the playground taunt, "Your mother dresses you funny," and gone home and let Barbara pick out his clothes. It worked for his brother and dad.

—*How the Hell Did This Happen?* (2017)

BUSINESS

You might think big business would be hard to define in this day of leveraged finances and interlocking technologies. Not so. Big business is every kind of business except the kind from which the person who's complaining about big business draws his pay.

—*Parliament of Whores* (1991)

When you looked at the Republicans you saw the scum off the top of business. When you looked at the Democrats you saw the scum off the top of politics. Personally, I prefer business.

—*Parliament of Whores* (1991)

BUSINESS INVESTMENT

Business investment defines civilization. Barbarians don't raise money through debt and equity. They raise money through stealing. (Although, during the boom in subprime mortgage lending it was sometimes difficult to tell the difference.)

—*Don't Vote—It Just Encourages the Bastards* (2010)

BUSINESSMEN

We have Jeff Bezos in a New Kids on the Block bomber jacket, Bill Gates outfitted in Mr. Rogers's sweaters and Gloria Steinem's old aviators and cutting his own hair, Elon Musk smoking pot on TV, and Richard Branson looking like the guy at the end of the bar muttering lines from *The Big Lebowski.*

—*A Cry from the Far Middle* (2020)

CALIFORNIA

There are branches of my family too loony even for jobs in government. Now imagine that my family occupies hundreds of thousands of square miles and is made up of tens of millions of people too loony even for jobs in government. It's California.

—*Don't Vote—It Just Encourages the Bastards* (2010)

California cuisine in perfection: My chicken had not only been allowed to range free, it had been given aromatherapy and stress counseling.

—*Eat the Rich* (1998)

CHICKEN LITTLE

You can almost hear Chicken Little's New Hampshire primary speech. "My feathered friends, our coops are guarded by foxes! All our eggs are in one basket! We're living on chicken feed! Massive layoffs are threatened at KFC! Plus, the sky is falling! In these troubled times, who better to lead us in squawking and fluttering and running around after our heads have been cut off than the Honorable C. Little—a real *chicken*!"

—*Age and Guile Beat Youth, Innocence, and
a Bad Haircut* (1995)

CHICKEN LITTLE'S AGENDA

Was Chicken Little running around telling all the other chickens that the sky was falling out of pure, disinterested altruism? Or was there something Chicken Little wanted? And once Chicken Little had all the other chickens convinced that the sky was falling was there, all of a sudden, a Federal Department of Falling Sky? And did Chicken Little get appointed Secretary of Things That Hit You on the Head?

—*Age and Guile Beat Youth, Innocence, and
a Bad Haircut* (1995)

CIVIL RIGHTS

We applaud the outcome of the Civil War and the civil rights movement, but an alternative—less costly in blood and treasure—was to not treat Black people like shit for five hundred years.

—*Don't Vote—It Just Encourages the Bastards* (2010)

CIVIL WAR

Of course these internal political contretemps can get out of hand. The Civil War comes to mind. However, as heated as America's arguments may be at the moment, this is not 1861. Ft. Sumter is not taking any incoming. Our political battles are all smoke and no lethal fire. (Except from a few fringe lunatics, of course. But we've always had those.)

—*A Cry from the Far Middle* (2020)

THE CLINTONS

"Mind your own business and keep your hands to yourself." These may be rightly called the Bill and Hillary Clinton Rules. Hillary, mind your own business. Bill, keep your hands to yourself.

—*Don't Vote—It Just Encourages the Bastards* (2010)

That fat kid who played saxophone in the school band and told on us when we were smoking in the boys' room—him and his wife, the Iron Dingbat, don't even drive a car. They ride around in the back of long, black tax tractors fogging the windows with damp exhalations about reinventing government.

—*Age and Guile Beat Youth, Innocence, and*
a Bad Haircut (1995)

Bill Clinton was an ancient monument of liberalism. If Washington were Pharaonic Egypt—and sometimes it is—Hillary would be the Sphinx. With the exception that she never shuts up. And she's hardly immobile. For the past quarter of a century she's been everywhere we looked.

—*How the Hell Did This Happen?* (2017)

THE CLINTONS (ADMINISTRATION)

Bill Clinton was able to harness warmongering's increase in political power and prestige without losing the support of smug lefty pacifists. He was Franklin Delano Gandhi.

—*The CEO of the Sofa* (2001)

The Clinton administration is going to decrease government spending by increasing the amount of money we give to the government to spend.

—*Age and Guile Beat Youth, Innocence, and*
a Bad Haircut (1995)

Mrs. Clinton is oblivious to the idea that the government programs she advocates may have caused the problems the government programs she advocates are supposed to solve.

—*The CEO of the Sofa* (2001)

THE CLINTONS (LITTLE ROCK)

Little Rock by day isn't much fun for anyone. There's nobody on the downtown streets. The city has that dead look of places where people make their money behind closed doors. Every third building seems to be a lawyer's office. The Rose Law Firm occupies a whole block. Its windows are dark. The curtains don't move. It's a sinister place in a friendly, red brick colonial way, as though the Continental Congress had a Ministry of Fear.

—Age and Guile Beat Youth, Innocence,
and a Bad Haircut (1995)

THE CLINTONS (SEX LIVES)

A lot of people say that Hillary's healthcare reform plan almost destroyed Bill Clinton's first term. It certainly diminished Hillary's influence in the White House. Bill had to seek help from a different woman to almost destroy his second term.

—Don't Vote—It Just Encourages the Bastards (2010)

COMMITTEES

Given the complete dominance of politics by Committee Brain, the wonder is that anything gets done, and the horror is that it does. What government accomplishes is what you'd expect from a committee. "A camel is a horse designed by a committee" is a saying that couldn't be more wrong. A camel is a seeing-eye dog designed by a committee

and available free with government grants to the halt and
the lame.

*—Don't Vote—It Just Encourages
the Bastards* (2010)

COMMUNISTS

The redskis have infiltrated the all-important exercise-video
industry, not to mention movies and TV. Academia, too, is a veri-
table compost heap of Bolshie brainmulch. Beardo the Weirdo
may have been laughed out of real life during the 1970s but he
found a home in our nation's colleges, where he whiles away the
wait for the next Woodstock Nation by pestering undergraduates
with collectivist twaddle when they should be thinking about
better car stereos.

—The Enemies List (1996)

Communism appealed to the kind of progressive intellectuals who liked to read dinosaur-turd sonnets while sitting on
Bauhaus ass-crampers inside Le Corbusier terrariums lit by
yard-sale lamps.

—The CEO of the Sofa (2001)

Enormous differences in income, wealth, and power push
people toward communism. And maybe so, but the only people
it pushed toward communism in America were sixties college
students who already had income, wealth, and power—or at
least their fathers did.

—Eat the Rich (1998)

For young people today, the only communist societies they know anything about are that goofy outlier North Korea and Cuba where the Marxist-Leninism comes with cheap rum, '57 Chevys, and "Guantanamera" sing-alongs.

—*A Cry from the Far Middle* (2020)

Communists are now just another small, half-baked cult who put out an occasional newsletter (the *Washington Post,* for instance) and pester people in airports (particularly Peking's).

—*The Enemies List* (1996)

CONGRESS

When buying and selling are controlled by legislation, the first things to be bought and sold are legislators.

—*Parliament of Whores* (1991)

CONSERVATION

When we gather in a big public crowd, we want the political system to do something. If we wanted to do something ourselves, we'd be at work. If we wanted to learn something, we'd be at school. And if we were really interested in natural resource conservation, we'd conserve some resources by staying home.

—*The CEO of the Sofa* (2001)

CONSERVATIVES

Conservatives can be buttheads, too. There are the reborn Jesus creeps, for instance. We should do to these what the conservative Romans did, with lions. But even regular country club–type Republicans can be stuffy about some things—dope smuggling, for example, and mixing Quaaludes in your scotch, and putting your stereo speakers on the roof of your house and turning the volume all the way up and playing Parliament of Funk at 3:00 A.M.
—*Republican Party Reptile* (1987)

CONSPIRACY THEORIES

The presidential "Birther," the 9/11 "Truther," the JFK assassination "Grassy Knoller," and every other conspiracy buff is announcing aloud: "The world is so stupid that even I can understand it."
—*Don't Vote—It Just Encourages the Bastards* (2010)

All conspiracy theories are based on the assumptions that, first, any group of people numbering two or more can agree on anything for longer than it takes to get another beer from the refrigerator and, second, that they'll keep their mouths shut.
—*Don't Vote—It Just Encourages the Bastards* (2010)

THE CONSTITUTION

Article One, Section 9, paragraph 7 of the U.S. Constitution says, "No money shall be drawn from the Treasury, but in consequence of appropriations made by law. . . ." So it's obvious what the whole point of lawmaking is.

—*Parliament of Whores* (1991)

CONSTITUTIONAL AMENDMENTS

The message of the Ninth and Tenth Amendments is: You have other rights but you have to guess what they are.

—*Don't Vote—It Just Encourages the Bastards* (2010)

CORPORATE LEADERSHIP

If you want to get one of those great red beefy, impressive-looking faces that politicians and corporation presidents have, you had better start drinking early and stick with it.

—*Modern Manners* (1983)

TED CRUZ

A skinny suit is wrong for people with big feet or wearing cowboy boots like Ted Cruz. In cropped pants with six-inch leg openings, Ted would look like he was stalking the corridors of power in cowhide water skis.

—*How the Hell Did This Happen?* (2017)

CULTURE WARS

Republicans are still fighting the culture wars, dug in on the front lines and courageously blazing away, never mind that the enemy has declared victory and gone home to celebrate with legalized marijuana at a same-sex wedding reception.

—*How the Hell Did This Happen?* (2017)

THE DEATH PENALTY

The Democrats were for a lot more of something to be named at a later date. The Republicans were for less of whatever it was except the death penalty.

—*Parliament of Whores* (1991)

Democrats believe in killing babies and old people, and, to judge by their various plans to modify American medical care, they believe in killing everyone else too. Except for murderers.

—*The CEO of the Sofa* (2001)

DEBT

Subordinated debt is not money that the bank has. It's money that the bank has borrowed from somebody else, maybe you. In other words, the money that you have deposited in a bank is guaranteed by money that you've loaned the bank plus money that you've deposited in the bank, which the bank owes you back, plus a parking lot.

"Hello, mattress. Meet my savings."

—*None of My Business* (2018)

THE DECLARATION OF INDEPENDENCE

It should be noted that the Declaration of Independence reads, "Life, Liberty, and the Pursuit of Happiness," not, "Life, Liberty, and Whoopee."

> —*Don't Vote—It Just Encourages the Bastards* (2010)

DEMOCRACY

We're a democracy—except occasionally in Florida during electoral college vote recounts.

> —*Peace Kills* (2004)

Our democracy, our culture, our whole way of life is a spectacular triumph of the blah. . . . Maybe our national mindlessness is the very thing that keeps us from turning into one of those smelly European countries full of pseudo reds and crypto-fascists and greens who dress like forest elves. So what if I don't agree with the Democrats? What's to disagree with? They believe everything. And what they don't believe, the Republicans do. Neither of them stands for anything they believe in, anyway. And from this, we've built a great nation.

> —*Parliament of Whores* (1991)

It is remarkable, on close inspection, what a lousy way to get things done democracy is. Not that democracy necessarily makes the wrong decisions. Private enterprise can do this with equal or greater ease. But in a democracy the decision-making process must be listened to. The great thing about the invisible hand of the market is not that it's invisible but that it's silent.

—*Parliament of Whores* (1991)

DEMOCRATS AND REPUBLICANS

We had a choice between Democrats who couldn't learn from the past and Republicans who couldn't stop living in it.

—*Parliament of Whores* (1991)

Democrats are the party of government activism, the party that says government can make you richer, smarter, taller and get the chickweed out of your lawn. Republicans are the party that says government doesn't work, and then they get elected and prove it.

—*Parliament of Whores* (1991)

Democrats are too busy trying to figure out a way to take all the money away from Republicans and give it to the government so that government can do all the work while Democrats go to the gym.

—*How the Hell Did This Happen?* (2017)

If a Republican won, conservatism would flow freely again, a mighty Mississippi of entrepreneurial initiative and individual responsibility with a lot of muddy corruption at the bottom. Meanwhile, the American public wasn't holding either political party in much esteem. What the American public was holding was its nose.

—*How the Hell Did This Happen?* (2017)

The Democrats said, "We don't know what's wrong with America, but we can fix it." The Republicans said, "There's nothing wrong with America, and we can fix that."

—*Parliament of Whores* (1991)

When Republicans ruin the environment, destroy the supply of affordable housing, and wreck the industrial infrastructure, at least they make a buck off it. The Democrats just do these things for fun.

—*Parliament of Whores* (1991)

What Americans don't understand about Republicans, and what causes a lot of Americans to continue to be Democrats, is that Republicans don't *want* anybody to become Republican. This is because it's already hell getting a tee time.

—*The CEO of the Sofa* (2001)

The Democrats planned to fiddle while Rome burned. The Republicans were going to burn Rome, then fiddle.

—*Parliament of Whores* (1991)

DRUG ABUSE

Drugs are just too good as a political issue. Drug abuse is one of those home-and-mother oratorical points that let politicians bray without fear of offending any powerful lobbying groups, unless they're running for President of Colombia. Nobody except Timothy Leary and me at about four in the morning is going to say a word in defense of illegal drugs.

—*Give War a Chance* (1992)

The scientists studying drugs are getting their money from the politicians who made drugs illegal.

—*The CEO of the Sofa* (2001)

THE EDUCATIONAL SYSTEM

The "failing American educational system" is mostly failing those Americans who think they are too smart to pay attention in school.

—*Parliament of Whores* (1991)

EFFICIENCY EXPERTS

Central planning always looks efficient and expert—from a distance. But central planning always ends up with an "efficiency expert" deciding it would be more efficient if everyone wore the same size underpants, selected by an expert. I am hoping, for my sake, that that expert doesn't come over from the private sector at, say, Victoria's Secret. A *thong?* That's wrong.

—*None of My Business* (2018)

ELECTIONS

Nearly half of all Americans with a vote have used it in past elections, often with tragic results.

—*Don't Vote—It Just Encourages the Bastards* (2010)

In order to get elected, a politician has to claim that the government can make you richer, smarter, taller, better looking and take six strokes off your golf game. And he has to claim that government can do all these things for free or, at least, very cheaply. As a result of these various factors, politicians are—and I'd like to put this as kindly as possible—lying, ignorant bums.

—*The Enemies List* (1996)

You're only allowed to have real ideas if it's absolutely guaranteed that you can't win an election.

—*Parliament of Whores* (1991)

Running for office is fundamentally a matter of telling untruths.

—*The Enemies List* (1996)

ELECTIONS (PRIMARIES)

The primaries have different rules depending on your location. It's a baseball game where if you're on first base you're supposed to dunk the ball through the net, if you're on second base you're supposed to knock the puck past the goalie, and if you're on third base you're supposed to kick a field goal.

—*How the Hell Did This Happen?* (2017)

To call our system of primaries and party caucuses a beauty contest is to slander the Miss America pageant.

—*Parliament of Whores* (1991)

ENVIRONMENTAL CONSCIOUSNESS

It is sometimes thought that Republicans are not environmentally conscious, that we are not concerned about the planet or, as we call it, the outdoors. This is not true. We love the outdoors and carefully instruct our children in its manifold splendors. For example, the son of a Republican friend of mine, when asked by his preschool teacher if he could name the four seasons, proudly said, "Dove, ducks, deer, and quail!"

—Holidays in Heck (2011)

FAMILY CARS

What Americans with children want is something that can be run through the car wash with the windows open (and maybe with the urchins left inside). While we're at it, please let's go back to simple, sturdy lap belts in the middle of rear bench seats. An engineering degree is required to rig an infant seat in a shoulder harness. If it isn't done right, and you leave a window open, you can find that the inertia locks have played out and that seat and scion are flapping outside in the breeze.

—Driving Like Crazy (2009)

FARM POLICY

U.S. farm policy is, along with North Korea and the Stanford liberal arts faculty, one of the world's last outposts of anti-free-market dogmatism.

—Parliament of Whores (1991)

U.S. farm policy, besides not doing what it's supposed to, does do what it isn't supposed to, and lots of it—the law of unintended consequences being one piece of legislation Congress always passes.

—*Parliament of Whores* (1991)

THE FAT LADY SINGING

It *is* over when the fat lady sings. Politics has become an obese operatic performer, warbling so loudly that none of us bit players can be heard, and so fat that we're shoved into the orchestra pit.

—*How the Hell Did This Happen?* (2017)

FEMINISM

Miniskirts caused feminism. Women wore miniskirts. Construction workers made ape noises. Women got pissed off. Once the women were pissed off about this they started thinking about all the other things they had to be pissed off about. That led to feminism. Not that I'm criticizing. Look, Babe . . . I mean, Ms . . . I mean, yes, sir, I *do* support feminism. I really do. But that doesn't mean I want to go through it twice.

—*Age and Guile Beat Youth, Innocence, and a Bad Haircut* (1995)

FENCE-SITTING

Bring the Wishy and the Washy back together, along with the Namby and the Pamby, and the Milk and the Toast. We may be on different sides of the fence but let's make that fence top wider and better padded and then go sit on it.

—*A Cry from the Far Middle* (2020)

FOOD

I had a lion steak once, at a German restaurant in, of all places, Springfield, Massachusetts. The flavor was of militant liver.

—*Eat the Rich* (1998)

The food sold on Calcutta's streets may be unidentifiable, but it's less likely than New York City hot dogs to contain a cow rectum.

—*The CEO of the Sofa* (2001)

FOREIGN POLICY

Whatever it is that the government does, sensible Americans would prefer that the government do it to somebody else. This is the idea behind foreign policy.

—*Parliament of Whores* (1991)

Maybe it's understandable what a history of failures America's foreign policy has been. We are, after all, a country full of people who came to America to get away from foreigners.

—*Parliament of Whores* (1991)

THE FOUNDING FATHERS

Considering the shiftless, slave-trading, bed-hopping, debt-ducking (and that's just Thomas Jefferson) nature of America's founding fathers, who also included rum-soaked bunkum merchants and Indian-massacring land swindlers (and they all oppressed women and weren't vegans) we should be careful about saying that certain societies or nationalities or religious persuasions aren't "ready for democracy."

—*Don't Vote—It Just Encourages the Bastards* (2010)

FRANKENSTEIN

When Dr. Frankenstein is up to something in his castle, does modern America send the county building inspector to check if the electrical wiring is safe? Not when a large group of activists with pitchforks and torches are available to chase Dr. Frankenstein back to the local urgent care facility and make him provide Medicare for All.

—*A Cry from the Far Middle* (2020)

FREE CAPITAL MORALITY

The people who are harmed most by free capital are people who are operating at a disadvantage. Being kind to the disadvantaged is a core principle of morality. You wouldn't trip a blind man. But, somehow, government thinks it's all right to go to the neighborhood where the blind man lives and take all the sewer grates off the storm sewers and all the manhole covers off the manholes.

—*None of My Business* (2018)

FREEDOM OF ASSEMBLY

Freedom of assembly is important—if you're going to an assembly. Most people are going to the mall. And, at the mall, they exercise economic freedom.

—*Don't Vote—It Just Encourages the Bastards* (2010)

FREE ENTERPRISE

As I floated in the pool, a gin fizz balanced on my paunch, I reflected that a liking for free enterprise, civil society, and material comforts as opposed to a liking for august institutions of democratic government indicated that none of my family will stray far from the GOP verities of life.

—*Holidays in Heck* (2011)

THE FREE MARKET

The free market is a bathroom scale. We may not like what we see when we step on the bathroom scale, but we can't pass a law making ourselves weigh 165.

—*Don't Vote—It Just Encourages the Bastards* (2010)

Yes, there's competition in free markets. That's what makes them work. Competition is the vermouth in the martini. But as it is with martinis, so it is with free markets. For every one part competition vermouth there are six parts of that top shelf gin called spontaneous cooperation among free people. (Which always seems to leave politicians "shaken, not stirred.")

> —*A Cry from the Far Middle* (2020)

Adam Smith pointed it out, 244 years ago: Among free people, in a free market exchange of goods and services, everyone comes out ahead. Each person gives something he or she values less in return for something he or she values more. Both sides win. I've got the Grey Goose. You've got the Noilly Prat, the olives, and the crushed ice. Bottoms up!

> —*A Cry from the Far Middle* (2020)

FREE SPEECH

Free speech should not only be protected, it should be compulsory.

> —*A Cry from the Far Middle* (2020)

Freedom of speech is important—if you have anything to say. I've checked the Internet; nobody does.

> —*Don't Vote—It Just Encourages the Bastards* (2010)

Everyone with a strong political opinion should be required to wear a sign proclaiming it. Hang an "Immigration Is Ruining

America" placard around your neck and see how you get treated by restaurant staff, Uber drivers, the people who change your hotel linen, and your immigrant grandparents. Go see your personal physician with "I Want the Government to Run Your Doctor's Office" lettered in Magic Marker across your abdomen. "Sorry, Senator Warren, but it looks like we're going to have to remove your *other* appendix."

—*A Cry from the Far Middle* (2020)

GOD IS A REPUBLICAN, AND SANTA CLAUS IS A DEMOCRAT

God is an elderly or, at any rate, middle aged male, a stern fellow, patriarchal rather than paternal and a great believer in rules and regulations. He holds men strictly accountable for their actions. He has little apparent concern for the material well-being of the disadvantaged. He is politically connected, socially powerful and holds the mortgage on literally everything in the world. God is difficult. God is unsentimental. It is very hard to get into God's heavenly country club.

Santa Claus is another matter. He's cute. He's nonthreatening. He's always cheerful. And he loves animals. He may know who's been naughty and who's been nice, but he never does anything about it. He gives everyone everything they want without thought of a quid pro quo. He works hard for charities, and he's famously generous to the poor. Santa Claus is preferable to God in every way but one: There is no such thing as Santa Claus.

—*Parliament of Whores* (1991)

THE GOLD STANDARD

There are people who think we should go back on the gold standard, and not all of them have skinny sideburns, large belt buckles, and live on armed compounds in Idaho. Money ought to be worth *something*, and gold seems as good as whatever.

—Eat the Rich (1998)

GOVERNMENT

Giving money and power to government is like giving whiskey and car keys to teenage boys.

—Parliament of Whores (1991)

The most sensible request we make of government is not "Do something!" but "Quit it!"

—Don't Vote—It Just Encourages the Bastards (2010)

A little government and a little luck are necessary in life, but only a fool trusts either of them.

—Parliament of Whores (1991)

Feeling good about government is like looking on the bright side of any catastrophe. When you quit looking on the bright side, the catastrophe is still there.

—Parliament of Whores (1991)

The government gives so much money to jerks that giving money to jerks must be—like giving the power to set the national agenda to network TV—one of the basic, constitutionally mandated purposes of government.

—*Parliament of Whores* (1991)

Government isn't a philosophical concept, it's a utility, a service industry—a way to get roads built and have Iraqis killed.

—*Give War a Chance* (1992)

If government were a product, selling it would be illegal. Government is a health hazard. Governments have killed many more people than cigarettes or unbuckled seat belts ever have. Government contains impure ingredients—as anybody who's looked at Congress can tell you.

—*Age and Guile Beat Youth, Innocence, and a Bad Haircut* (1995)

To debate government policy using only reason is to ignore a number of important irrational aspects of government.

—*Parliament of Whores* (1991)

The government is a rottweiler ready to be unleashed on your problems. And you've stuffed raw meat down the front of your pants.

—*Don't Vote—It Just Encourages the Bastards* (2010)

LINDSEY GRAHAM

Lindsey Graham's strategy was to have a girl's name, tricking progressives into thinking they were voting for America's first transgender president.

—*How the Hell Did This Happen?* (2017)

GREEN

The Green dweebs want a world where individuals don't count for much, where all the important decisions—such as whether to shift the Viper into fifth—are made in Washington. They want a world controlled by the political process. That's because the shrub cuddlers are, as individuals, so insignificant. They're losers, the three-bong-hit saviors of the earth, lava lamp luddites, global warming dolts, ozone boneheads, peace creeps, tofu twinks, Birkenstock buttinskis, and bed-wetting vegetarian bicyclists who bother whales on weekends. They have no money, sense, or skills. But they can make their mark on politics because the whole idea of politics is to achieve power without possessing merit.

—*Age and Guile Beat Youth, Innocence, and a Bad Haircut* (1995)

GUN CONTROL

There are important arguments in favor of gun ownership. What with the economy being like it is, I call my .38 Special "the MasterCard of the future."

—*Don't Vote—It Just Encourages the Bastards* (2010)

One extremely important thing about Republicans. We're against gun control. You can shoot us.

—*Age and Guile Beat Youth, Innocence,
and a Bad Haircut* (1995)

HARVARD

Wouldn't it be swell to be on the Crimson gravy train? I'd probably be a government big shot by now, undermining U.S. foreign policy, or a CEO running some industry into the ground. I'd have that wonderful accent like I'd put the Fix-A-Dent on the wrong side of my partial plate. And I'd have lots of high-brow Ivy League friends. We could have drinks at the Harvard Club and show off our Ivy League ability to get loud on one gin fizz.

—*Holidays in Hell* (1988)

There, but for low high school grades, middling SAT scores, a horrible disciplinary record and parents with less than $100 in the bank, go I. How sad.

—*Holidays in Hell* (1988)

Harvard *is* the home of American ideas; there have been several of these, and somebody has to take the blame for them. But it ain't the likes of me. Us yokels who majored in beer and getting the skirts off Tri-Delts bear no responsibility for Thoreau's hippie jive or John Kenneth Galbraith's nitwit economics or Henry Kissinger's brown-nosing the Shah of Iran.

—*Holidays in Hell* (1988)

HAWAII

Hawaii has so much scenery it's a wonder Congress hasn't passed scenic quota legislation and bused some of these views to Nebraska.

—*Age and Guile Beat Youth, Innocence, and a Bad Haircut* (1995)

The Big Island, Hawaii proper, is the place where migrating Polynesians originally landed more than 1,500 years ago and where Captain Cook died in 1779. Cook was the first *haole* (a Hawaiian word meaning "person whose luggage is still at the Los Angeles airport") to visit Hawaii. His crew spread venereal disease through the islands, the Hawaiians beat Captain Cook to death with clubs, and the tourist trade has continued with only minor alterations to the present day.

—*Age and Guile Beat Youth, Innocence, and a Bad Haircut* (1995)

After dinner three sensitive and intelligent young ladies with their shirts off performed the *hula*, an ancient Hawaiian folk dance which tells the story of three sensitive and intelligent young ladies with their shirts off who have too many strategically placed shell necklaces and cannot quite shake them loose although they try very hard. I found this important cultural event very artistic and absorbing.

—*Age and Guile Beat Youth, Innocence, and a Bad Haircut* (1995)

HEALTH CARE

Health care is too expensive, so the Clinton administration is putting a high-powered corporate lawyer—Hillary—in charge

of making it cheaper. (This is what I always do when I want to spend less money—hire a lawyer from Yale.)
   —*Age and Guile Beat Youth, Innocence, and a Bad Haircut* (1995)

If you think health care is expensive now, wait until you see what it costs when it's free.
   —*Age and Guile Beat Youth, Innocence, and a Bad Haircut* (1995)

Something doesn't add up. Politicians are telling me that I can smoke, drink, gain two hundred pounds, then win an iron man triathlon at age ninety-five.
   —*Don't Vote—It Just Encourages the Bastards* (2010)

HISTORY

Just ask Americans a question about American history, watch them draw a blank, and you'll see that we are the happy people indeed.
   —*Don't Vote—It Just Encourages the Bastards* (2010)

INSURRECTION

The war is not between Republicans and Democrats or between conservatives and progressives. The war is between the frightened and what they fear. It is being fought by the people who perceive themselves as controlling nothing. They are besieging the people they perceive as controlling everything. We are in

the midst of a Perception Insurrection, or, depending on how
you perceive it, a Loser Mutiny.
                              —*How the Hell Did This Happen?* (2017)

INVESTMENT BANKS

There's a sign on the door at most New York investment banks:
NO SHIRT, NO SHOES, NO IPO.
                              —*The CEO of the Sofa* (2001)

ISOLATIONISM

Americans would like to ignore foreign policy. Our previous
attempts at isolationism were successful. Unfortunately, they
were successful for Hitler's Germany and Tojo's Japan.
                              —*Peace Kills* (2004)

IT TAKES A VILLAGE

Nearly everything about *It Takes a Village* is objectionable,
from the title—an ancient African proverb that seems to
have its origins in the ancient African kingdom of Hallmark-
cardia—to the acknowledgments page where Mrs. Clinton fails
to acknowledge that some poor journalism professor named
Barbara Feinman did most of the work.
                              —*The CEO of the Sofa* (2001)

The totalitarianism in *It Takes a Village* is of a namby-pamby, eat-your-vegetables kind that doesn't so much glorify the state and nation as pester the dickens out of them.

—*The CEO of the Sofa* (2001)

It takes a village to raise a child. The village is Washington. You are the child.

—*The CEO of the Sofa* (2001)

THE KNOW-NOTHINGS

At least the members of the Know-Nothing Party knew they knew nothing.

—*How the Hell Did This Happen?* (2017)

LAISSEZ-FAIRE

Should the government be Laissez? Or should the government be Faire?

—*A Cry from the Far Middle* (2020)

LAW AND ORDER AND WEATHER

Half the year we have floods and droughts and depressed prices on the commodities market and the rest of the time we have drug smuggling, extortion, murder, and theft.

—*Republican Party Reptile* (1987)

LEGALIZING DRUGS

Legalizing drugs will lower their price, the more so if price is measured not only in dollars but also in time spent with dangerous maniacs in dark parking lots, not to mention time spent in jail.

—*The CEO of the Sofa* (2001)

LIBERALISM

Liberalism is deeply confusing to liberals. America's first great liberal populist was Andrew Jackson, perpetrator of the genocidal Trail of Tears and annihilator of the Second Bank of the United States and hence of centralized economic control.

—*How the Hell Did This Happen?* (2017)

Classical Liberalism has had a good run. Now it's about to get run over by a bus full of stupid "post-capitalist" political trends—the new socialism, the new nationalism, the new trade war mercantilism, and the new social media platforms that drive this bus. Vladimir Putin, Xi Jinping, Donald Trump, and the numerous candidates who ran for the 2020 Democratic presidential nomination are all onboard. So are the Brexiteers and so, for that matter, are the maniacally micro-regulating bureaucrats of the EU that the Brexiteers want to leave.

—*A Cry from the Far Middle* (2020)

LIBERAL POLITICAL-ECONOMIC REASONING

Using liberal political-economic reasoning I can prove . . . *anything*. I can prove that shooting convenience-store clerks stimulates the economy. Jobs are created in the high-paying domestic manufacturing sector at gun and ammunition factories. Additional emergency medical technicians, security guards, health care providers, and morticians are hired. The unemployment rate is lowered as job seekers fill new openings on convenience-store night shifts. And money stolen from convenience-store cash registers stimulates the economy where stimulus is most needed, in low-income neighborhoods where the people who shoot convenience-store clerks go to buy their crack. I am simply flabbergasted that the Democratic majority in the House and Senate isn't smoking crack and shooting convenience-store clerks this very minute, considering all the good it does.

—*Don't Vote—It Just Encourages*
the Bastards (2010)

LIBERALS

The liberal is trying to fix my wristwatch with a ballpeen hammer.

—*The Enemies List* (1996)

The principal feature of contemporary American liberalism is sanctimoniousness.

—*Give War a Chance* (1992)

The danger with political issues, for liberals, is that you might try to understand them.

—The CEO of the Sofa (2001)

Liberals are fond of victims and seek them wherever they go. The more victimized the better—the best victims being too ignorant and addled to challenge their benefactors. This is why animal rights is such an excellent liberal issue. Not even a Democratic presidential candidate is as ignorant and addled as a dead laboratory rat.

—Give War a Chance (1992)

Democrats are liberals, and—to their profound embarrassment—liberalism is an old, white European male political philosophy.

—How the Hell Did This Happen? (2017)

Everybody hates liberal Democrats these days. Of course, being good liberals, they hate themselves, too.

—The Enemies List (1996)

LIBERTARIANS

The libertarian creed of individual dignity, individual liberty, and individual responsibility comes with that responsibility kicker. And there's the *Atlas Shrugged* doorstop, which got some Baby Boomers all excited and the rest of us wondering who hid the Strunk and White.

—The Baby Boom (2014)

LUCKY SPERM SCHOLARSHIP SOCIETY

The Lucky Sperm Scholarship Society is a small privileged class of elite Americans who have shoe-size IQs and the best educations that money, power, and influence can buy. If George W. Bush and Al Gore had grown up on my block in Toledo, Ohio, they wouldn't have gone to Yale and Harvard. They would have gone to Kent State. Easy to picture them there circa 1970— Al picking up on the hippie thing a little late, ordering his bell-bottoms from the Sears catalog, and George W. in a *real* National Guard unit, shooting Al.

—*The CEO of the Sofa* (2001)

MAINE

Maine, where every river, lake, and mountain peak is named after an item of clothing from L. L. Bean.

—*Age and Guile Beat Youth, Innocence, and a Bad Haircut* (1995)

MASS MOVEMENTS

All those masses in the mass movement have to be called to action, and that call to action better be exciting, or the masses will lose interest and wander off to play arcade games.

—*Parliament of Whores* (1991)

There's a whiff of the lynch mob or the lemming migration about any overlarge concentration of like-thinking individuals, no matter how virtuous their cause. Even a band of angels can turn ugly and start looting if enough angels are unemployed and hanging around the pearly gates convinced that succubi own all the liquor stores in heaven.

—Parliament of Whores (1991)

MEDICARE

Does Medicare for All mean that young people have to wear trifocals and Depends and trade their bicycles for walkers?

—A Cry from the Far Middle (2020)

MIDDLE-CLASS RESENTMENT

Only rich kids with indulgent parents and poor kids with after-school jobs had their own cars. And thus began the political trend of Angry Middle-Class Resentment.

—The Baby Boom (2014)

MILITIAMEN

Militiamen call you a spy if you have a two-way radio, and also because the militiamen love two-way radios and calling you a spy at gunpoint is a good way to get a free one.

—Republican Party Reptile (1987)

MONEY

Getting people to give vast amounts of money when there's no firm idea what that money will do is like throwing maidens down a well. It's an appeal to magic. And the results are likely to be as stupid and disappointing as the results of magic usually are.

—*Give War a Chance* (1992)

Why's this soiled, crumpled, overdecorated piece of paper bearing a picture of a man who was something of a failure as a president worth $50?

—*None of My Business* (2018)

Kings, emperors, and even lowly congressional representatives have expenses. It is to a government's advantage to pay for those expenses with funny money. One reason that the concept of money so often violates common sense is that governments so often do crazy things with money.

—*None of My Business* (2018)

Money is to politicians what the eucalyptus tree is to koala bears: food, water, shelter, and something to crap on.

—*Eat the Rich* (1998)

NEW ENGLAND

In some rural places the most prominent citizen is the doctor or the reverend at the church; not so in New England.

It's the plumber, and for good reason. When your water pipes freeze and burst at 3:00 A.M., try calling an M.D. or a priest.

—*Republican Party Reptile* (1987)

NEW HAMPSHIRE

Pastoral serenity is elusive where every man, woman, and child over five owns a chain saw and starts it promptly at dawn each day.

—*Republican Party Reptile* (1987)

The state motto of New Hampshire seems to be "Can I freshen that up for you?"

—*Republican Party Reptile* (1987)

If you go jogging, people will stop and offer you a ride.

—*Republican Party Reptile* (1987)

RICHARD NIXON

Nixon looked like a grown-up, from a distance. Up close he looked like a grown-up reanimated by voodoo. He was so zoned out that he wore a suit and tie to go for a barefoot walk on a beach. But at least he was trying.

—*How the Hell Did This Happen?* (2017)

PEACE

We're all in favor of peace, but when the wolf dwells with the lamb and the leopard lies down with the kid, how often do we have to replace those sheep and goats?

—*A Cry from the Far Middle* (2020)

POLITICAL CAMPAIGNS

If taxpayer money is used to pay for political campaigns, do taxpayers have ninety days to return politicians for a full refund? Will the politicians still have to be in their original packaging?

—*A Cry from the Far Middle* (2020)

The campaigns have been all about being different from President Obama. Some candidates said, "I'm more right-wing!" Some candidates said, "I'm more left-wing!" But every candidate has said, in the language of his or her clothing, "I'm dumpier!"

—*How the Hell Did This Happen?* (2017)

POLITICAL PROMISES

Of course politicians don't tell the truth: "I am running for the U.S. Senate in order to even the score with those grade-school classmates of mine who, thirty-five years ago, gave me the nickname Fish Face," or, "Please elect me to Congress so that I can get out of the Midwest and meet bigwigs and cute babes."

—*Parliament of Whores* (1991)

But neither do politicians tell huge, entertaining whoppers: "Why, send yours truly to Capitol Hill, and I'll ship the swag home in boxcar lots. You'll be paving the roads with bacon around here when I get done shoveling out the pork barrel. There'll be government jobs for your dog. Leave your garden hose running for fifteen minutes, and I'll have the Department of Transportation build an eight-lane suspension bridge across the puddle. Show me a wet basement, and I'll get you a naval base and make your Roto-Rooter man an admiral of the fleet. There'll be farm subsidies for every geranium you've got in a pot, defense contracts for Junior's spitballs and free day care for Sister's dolls. You'll get unemployment for the sixteen hours every day when you're not at your job, full disability benefits if you have to get up in the night to take a leak, and Social Security checks will come in the mail not just when you retire at sixty-five but when you retire each night to bed. Taxes? Hell, I'll have the government go around every week putting money *back* in your paycheck, and I'll make the IRS hire chimpanzees from the zoo to audit your tax returns. Vote for me, folks, and you'll be farting through silk."

—*Parliament of Whores* (1991)

POLITICAL TENDENCIES

In America, instead of political parties, we have two vague political tendencies. One tendency is to favor a larger, more powerful government to make things better. The other tendency is to favor a smaller, more limited government to make things less worse.

—*How the Hell Did This Happen?* (2017)

POLITICIANS

Career politicians—especially in the House of Representatives—tend to be elected by pressure groups that dominate their constituencies. If the pressure group elects Clarabell and Clarabell limits out, the pressure group will elect Bozo. And when Bozo can't run anymore, Pennywise from It will be ushered into political office.

—*None of My Business* (2018)

Politicians never spend our tax money, they *invest* it. They've invested a lot of it. And they've been investing it for a long time. These must be very bad investments—or everybody in America would be rich by now.

—*How the Hell Did This Happen?* (2017)

Politicians don't fix scientific and economic problems. The last time political types were totally in charge of scientific research and economic planning they built the Chernobyl nuclear plant.

—*The CEO of the Sofa* (2001)

Politicians are always searching for some grave alarm which will cause individuals to abandon their separate concerns and prerogatives and act in concert so that politicians can wield the baton. Remember the War on Poverty? And how Jimmy Carter asked Americans to respond to a mere rise in the price of crude oil with "the moral equivalent of war"? (What were we supposed to do, shame the gas station attendant to death?)

—*All the Trouble in the World* (1994)

Distracting a politician from governing is like distracting a bear from eating your baby. Or like getting a dog to quit chewing on your wallet.

—*Age and Guile Beat Youth, Innocence, and a Bad Haircut* (1995)

POLITICS

Just imagine politics with its dumbbell element subtracted. There would be no Republican candidates. There would be no Democratic voters. The whole system would collapse.

—*The CEO of the Sofa* (2001)

The American political system is like a gigantic Mexican Christmas fiesta. Each political party is a huge piñata—a papier-mâché donkey, for example. The donkey is filled with full unemployment, low interest rates, affordable housing, comprehensive medical benefits, a balanced budget, and other goodies. The American voter is blindfolded and given a stick. The voter then swings the stick wildly in every direction, trying to hit a political candidate on the head and knock some sense into the silly bastard.

—*Parliament of Whores* (1991)

There's nothing more oily and cynical in politics than telling the truth.

—*Parliament of Whores* (1991)

Many of us have sons and daughters who will not get into medical school or start a business, join the military, learn a trade, raise a family, perform needful volunteer work, or do anything else that has even the slightest value to society such as follow a Phish tribute band around the country selling artisanal hacky sacks outside concert venues. These children we send into politics.

—How the Hell Did This Happen? (2017)

Politics pits one generation of Americans against another. The millennials are mad at the baby boomers for soaking up all the Social Security and Medicare gravy while, at the same time, refusing to retire, leaving the millennials to work in a "gig economy" where they make a living by driving each other around for Uber.

—A Cry from the Far Middle (2020)

Death is the result of bad politics.

—Give War a Chance (1992)

POLLUTION

Pollution occurs in the course of human enterprise. It is a by-product of people making things, things like a living.

—Parliament of Whores (1991)

It's rarely an identifiable person (and, of course, never you or me) who pollutes. It's a vague, sinister, faceless thing called industry.

—Parliament of Whores (1991)

POPULISM

We Americans like our populism in small doses and prefer-
ably from an elitist. A Democrat populist might mean what he
says and take our new Toro away because a family down the
street can't afford the self-starting kind with the de-thatching
attachment. A Republican populist is only going to indulge
in the popular types of populism and will then get back in
his Cadillac and behave.

—*Parliament of Whores* (1991)

POVERTY

Political systems must love poverty—they produce so much
of it.

—*Eat the Rich* (1998)

Democratic politicians care so much about poverty that—far
from warring on it—they have become a kind of conservation-
ist group, devoted to preserving it forever. Democrats are the
Sierra Club of Poverty.

—*How the Hell Did This Happen?* (2017)

POWER (DECENTRALIZATION)

The only effective way to keep power decentralized is by making sure our society provides ungovernmental ways of being
powerful. The biggest talents should be offered bait in places
other than Washington. Let the good and the great flounce

around in the arts, spout pious bilge from pulpits, fill the minds of the young with drivel at great universities, spread patronizing smarm through charitable organizations, and rob all comers in business. Just one ready, necessary thing is needed to set the hook in this lure of decentralization. Thank God for money.

—Don't Vote—It Just Encourages the Bastards (2010)

THE PRESIDENCY

If you want to get really depressed about the quality of our presidential hopefuls, think of it this way: What if you were wrongly accused of murder and any of these men showed up as your court-appointed attorney? Hello, lethal injection.

—Parliament of Whores (1991)

Every person in America has done or said something that would keep him or her from being president.

—Parliament of Whores (1991)

In our brief national history we have shot four of our presidents, worried five of them to death, impeached one and hounded another out of office. And when all else fails, we hold an election and assassinate their character.

—Parliament of Whores (1991)

Do you suppose the president understands how the computer codes that activate our nuclear arsenal work? When he opens the "football," will he be able to tell whether the stuff in there is real or whether it's just some readouts and LED displays slapped together by the Pentagon Art Department to look cool?

—*Parliament of Whores* (1991)

Whenever the authorities start meddling with ancient and customary traditions, something is wrong. So it was when President Jimmy Carter tried to put America on the metric system. And so it is today with an ancient and customary tradition we used to have, that the president of the United States was someone you would welcome into your home.

—*A Cry from the Far Middle* (2020)

PRESIDENTIAL ELECTIONS

Presidential candidates are selected by primary and caucus voters during a process that lasts longer than the life span of an average house pet. By the time we're done listening to all that endless squeaking of the exercise wheel inside the smelly cage of politics we're ready to smother the gerbil and fall asleep.

—*How the Hell Did This Happen?* (2017)

Show me one candidate who, like Millard Fillmore in 1856, has the honest decency to come right out and admit being a "Know-Nothing."

—*How the Hell Did This Happen?* (2017)

PRIVACY

We're on our way to a new life "Where Everybody Knows Your Name"—and your Social Security number, computer passwords, financial status, debit card PIN, credit rating, physical address, present whereabouts, etc. Everything about us will be seen and known. And my greatest fear is that when we arrive in this place of universal visibility and ubiquitous public knowledge of all our thoughts and deeds, we'll like it.

—*None of My Business* (2018)

A Security-and-Surveillance State that is all-seeing and all-knowing could replace religion. Something will. According to the Pew Research Center on Religion and Public Life, only about half of Americans age eighteen to twenty-nine are certain that they believe in any kind of God at all.

—*None of My Business* (2018)

PROBLEM-SOLVING

To be "doing something about the problem" is a fundamental American trait and by and large a good one. But, in our love of problem-solving, we sometimes forget to ask what the problem is or even whether it's a problem. And once we start doing something, we often lose sight of whether that something is the thing to do. I give you Vietnam, just for instance.

—*Give War a Chance* (1992)

RAINING ON PARADES

Raining on parades requires no skill or effort, which is what draws people into politics. All a politician needs is the upper-story window of public attention and the chamber pot of rhetoric.

—*Don't Vote—It Just Encourages the Bastards* (2010)

RONALD REAGAN

Ronald Reagan did presidential best. As an actor he was a pretty good politician, and his clothes were perfect. Central casting perfect. Technicolor perfect. Perfect beyond envy. You didn't want Reagan's clothes; you wanted a tub of buttered popcorn and a giant-sized soft drink.

—*How the Hell Did This Happen?* (2017)

I like Ronald Reagan, but the earth would be a happier planet if he hadn't been necessary.

—*Don't Vote—It Just Encourages the Bastards* (2010)

REDNECKS

Everyone in America has always wanted to be a redneck. That's why all those wig-and-knicker colonial guys moved to Kentucky with Davy Crockett even before he got his TV show. And witness aristocratic young Theodore Roosevelt's attempt to be a "rough rider." Even Henry James used the same last name as his peckerwood cousin Jesse. And as Henry James would tell you, if anyone read him anymore and also if he were still alive, the single most prominent distinguishing feature of the redneck is that he drives a pickup truck. This explains why all of us are muscling these things around downtown Minneapolis and Cincinnati.

—*Republican Party Reptile* (1987)

REPUBLICAN PARTY REPTILES

We are the Republican Party Reptiles. We look like Republicans, and think like conservatives, but we drive a lot faster and keep vibrators and baby oil and a video camera behind the stack of sweaters on the bedroom closet shelf.

—*Republican Party Reptile* (1987)

I think our agenda is clear. We are opposed to: government spending, Kennedy kids, seat-belt laws, being a pussy about nuclear power, busing our children anywhere other than Yale, trailer courts near our vacation homes, Gary Hart, all tiny Third World countries that don't have banking secrecy laws, aerobics, the U.N., taxation without tax loopholes, and jewelry on men. We are in favor of: guns, drugs, fast cars, free love (if our wives don't find out), a sound dollar, cleaner environment (poor people should cut it out with the graffiti), a strong military with spiffy uniforms, Nastassja Kinski, Star Wars (and anything else that scares the Russkis), and a firm stand on the Middle East (raze buildings, burn crops, plow the earth with salt, and sell the population into bondage). There are thousands of people in America who feel this way, especially after three or four drinks. If all of us would unite and work together, we could give this country . . . well, a real bad hangover.

—*Republican Party Reptile* (1987)

REPUBLICANS

I'm a registered Republican and consider socialism a violation of the American principle that you shouldn't stick your nose in other people's business except to make a buck.

—*Republican Party Reptile* (1987)

The very thought of naked Republicans should go a long way to curing America's obsession with the lewd.

—*The CEO of the Sofa* (2001)

THE SENATE

The Founding Fathers, in their wisdom, devised a method by which our republic can take one hundred of its most prominent numskulls and keep them out of the private sector, where they might do actual harm.

—*The CEO of the Sofa* (2001)

SMALL GOVERNMENT

We surrender certain of our natural liberties to a government of our own making in return for public safety and order.

Government is a necessary evil, and like all evils, however necessary, should be kept as small as possible.
                                    —*How the Hell Did This Happen?* (2017)

SOCIAL SECURITY

When the golden years begin there's always Social Security. I understand Meow Mix is one of the more palatable cat-food brands.
                                    —*Eat the Rich* (1998)

Unfortunate people who scrutinize the Social Security Trust Fund discover two facts: It's not there. It's not theirs.
                                    —*The CEO of the Sofa* (2001)

Social Security is a government program with a constituency made up of the old, the near-old and those who hope or fear to grow old. After 215 years of trying, we have finally discovered a special interest that includes 100 percent of the population. Now we can vote ourselves rich.
                                    —*Parliament of Whores* (1991)

Every political move to fix Social Security makes it worse.
                                    —*The CEO of the Sofa* (2001)

Government can't create a trust fund by saving its own IOUs any more than I could create a trust fund by writing *I get a chunk of cash when I turn twenty-one* on a piece of paper. Social

Security is just such a piece of paper, except it says, *I get a chunk of cash when I turn sixty-five, the government promises.* Consult American Indians for a fuller discussion of government promises.

—*The CEO of the Sofa* (2001)

SOCIETY

A peaceful society doesn't need as much political machinery as a society where everybody hates everybody's guts.

—*The CEO of the Sofa* (2001)

THE SOUTH

In the South you can still feel that loony American hybrid vigor and special USA camaraderie. The place is devoid of narcissistic personality disorders. It may be the "Me Generation" up north, but it's the "How You-All?" generation in the South.

—*Driving Like Crazy* (2009)

SOUTHERNERS

Nobody's eating roughage, running marathons, and taking yoga classes down there. People still drink, still smoke, still have guns, and still believe in a personal God who listens to *them.* They're not worried about the future. This country didn't come from people who worried about the future. It came from people who *whipped the future's ass.*

—*Driving Like Crazy* (2009)

SPECIAL INTERESTS

We usually think of "special interests" as being something out of a Thomas Nast cartoon—big men with cigars conspiring over a biscuit trust. But in fact, a special interest is any person or group that wants to be treated differently from the rest of us by the government.

—*Parliament of Whores* (1991)

The great danger of special interests is not that a minority of some kind will get fat at our nation's expense. The great danger is that our nation will discover a special interest to which a majority of us belong.

—*Parliament of Whores* (1991)

THE STOCK MARKET

The great surprise of the stock market is that it's a happy place—not only happy in a bull season, when everybody's making money, but also happy, in its way, when everything is falling apart. All free markets are mysterious in their behavior, but the New York Stock Exchange contains a mystery I never expected—transcendent bliss.

—*Eat the Rich* (1998)

That's our own money in the stock market, jumping up and down like a maniac on the price trampoline. Either we've made somersaulting investments of our own or pension funds and insurance companies have done it for us. We're worried our money is going to break its neck.

—*Eat the Rich* (1998)

So in order to understand the stock market, we have to realize that, like anything enormous and inert, it's fundamentally stable, and like anything emotion-driven, it's volatile as hell. Got that? Me neither.

—*Eat the Rich* (1998)

One of the old-fashioned charms of the NYSE, besides the littering, is the constant use of *fuck* as a noun, verb, adverb, and adjective with every possible meaning except "sexual intercourse."

—*Eat the Rich* (1998)

THE SUPREME COURT

For all we know, the Supreme Court decides cases by playing nude games of Johnny-on-a-pony.

—*Parliament of Whores* (1991)

TALKING TO EACH OTHER

Americans are acquiring more personal communication devices than there are persons. Walk into any public place and everyone is staring into a screen. There's no one to talk to. There's no longer any chance of striking up a friendly acquaintance in a waiting room, train, plane, or bar. Even when conversation does occur in a bar, the lively debate about who played shortstop for the 1986 Chicago Cubs is cut short by some fool Googling it. (Shawon Dunston.)

—*None of My Business* (2018)

TAXES

A businessman will steal from you directly instead of getting the IRS to do it for him.

—*Parliament of Whores* (1991)

Political power has grown in expense. One-third of the world's GDP is now spent by the politicians in governments. One out of every three things you make is grabbed by governments. If your cat has three kittens, one of them is a government agent.

—*How the Hell Did This Happen?* (2017)

TOLEDO, OHIO

There are also places in the world where the Jeep is worshipped as a totem of plenty, where Jeeps are icons in a sort of cargo cult, and the Wrangler is the deity of good wages, medical benefits, and retirement security. That would be in Toledo, Ohio, where the Jeep has been manufactured since its World War II conception, where Shriners muster fleets of

Jeepsters for each parade, where every third person seems to work at the Jeep plant.

—Driving Like Crazy (2009)

TOWN MEETINGS

A town meeting is tedious with that amazing and inexplicable tedium of a large number of people behaving themselves in public.

—Parliament of Whores (1991)

Taking part in a New England town meeting is like being a cell in a plant.

—Parliament of Whores (1991)

TRADE IMBALANCE

There is no such thing as a trade imbalance. Trade can't be out of balance because a balance is what trade is. Buyers and sellers decide that one thing is worth another. All free trade is balanced trade. Saying there's an imbalance in freely conducted trade is like saying there's an imbalance in freely conducted sex. It's like admitting you screwed some half-baked videographer who was hanging around your presidential campaign, and then claiming she had sex and you didn't.

—Don't Vote—It Just Encourages the Bastards (2010)

TRUMP

It's no fun making fun of Trump. The best humorists have given it their all trying to make him appear to be more foolish than he is. They've failed.

—*How the Hell Did This Happen?* (2017)

Trump was the guy from the mailroom who somehow wound up with a job interview for the position of National Sales Manager. If you promote him it will be a disaster. But if you leave him in the mailroom he'll take his pants down, sit on the Xerox machine, and fax the result to all your customers.

—*How the Hell Did This Happen?* (2017)

There's no such thing as a "Trumpist" ideology. The *ideo-* is lacking and so is the *-ology*, the "science" or "branch of knowledge" of which the President has not a twig. Trumpism can be explained in 140 characters on Twitter, and Trumpism can *only* be explained in 140 characters on Twitter. Try that with Marxism. QED.

—*How the Hell Did This Happen?* (2017)

The American government is of the people, by the people, for the people. And these days America is peopled by 320 million Donald Trumps.

—*How the Hell Did This Happen?* (2017)

Donald Trump is representative of all that we hold dear: money. Or, rather, he is representative of greed for money.

—*How the Hell Did This Happen?* (2017)

Trump has perfected the "I-don't-listen" look.

—*How the Hell Did This Happen?* (2017)

Trump isn't a real rich person. Trump is a fantasy rich person. When Trump's supporters see Trump they think, "That's me, in my dreams."

—*How the Hell Did This Happen?* (2017)

Trump's coif—I'm not going there. Too many have gone there before, including, it would seem, a family of angry squirrels who use Clairol. So I won't delve into the subject—for fear of angry squirrels.

—*How the Hell Did This Happen?* (2017)

TRUMP TOWER

Trump is like his Trump Tower, a hilarious building that looks like a giant bum chromed an accordion and is about to play Lawrence Welk tunes at Fifty-Seventh and Fifth for nickels and dimes.

—*How the Hell Did This Happen?* (2017)

TRUMP VS. HILLARY

Hillary is wrong about everything. She is to politics and statecraft what Pope Urban VIII and the Inquisition were to Galileo. She thinks the sun revolves around *herself.* But Trump Earth™ is flat. We'll sail over the edge. Here be monsters.

—*How the Hell Did This Happen?* (2017)

Hillary is a terrible *bien-pensant*, taking her opinions from the top of the social ladder she's been trying to climb since she was a teenager. In another time and place she'd be campaigning from Tara and with the slogan "Fiddle-Dee-Dee." Frankly, Hillary, I don't give a damn. I endorse you anyway.

—*How the Hell Did This Happen?* (2017)

Better a Marie Antoinette of the left saying, "Let them eat fruit and fiber" than a *sans-culotte* in Madame Defarge drag who would be Robespierre if he could spell it.

—*How the Hell Did This Happen?* (2017)

Better the devil you know than the devil who knows nothing. A devil who can't even figure out where the gates of hell are, and they've got his name right on them at Trump Tower.

—*How the Hell Did This Happen?* (2017)

TSA

Our original Security-and-Surveillance State was a state of grace—a oneness with God. Maybe a oneness with TSA will be just as good. Most Americans pass through airport security more often than they go to church. Comfort with Security-and-Surveillance runs even deeper in the human psyche than religion.

—*None of My Business* (2018)

VOTING

"Sit down and shut up" is how all important family discussions begin and end everywhere in America. America's family of voters applauds such concise statements of foreign and domestic policy goals.

—*How the Hell Did This Happen?* (2017)

I don't understand why the same newspaper commentators who bemoan the terrible education given to poor people are always so eager to have those poor people get out and vote.

—*Age and Guile Beat Youth, Innocence, and a Bad Haircut* (1995)

There are now more millennial voters than there are OK, Boomers. And they've got Uber to take them to the polls while I'm still trying to figure out how that app works and whether I should get into a car driven by someone who braids her beard.

—*A Cry from the Far Middle* (2020)

THE WAR ON DRUGS

Whom do you draft in a war against drugs? Certainly not eighteen-year-old boys. They're the enemy.

—*The CEO of the Sofa* (2001)

Drugs are a problem. We shouldn't stop worrying about the problem. But maybe we should start worrying about the solution.

—*Give War a Chance* (1992)

WASHINGTON, DC

Washington has lots of those Greek- and Roman-style build-ings that make you feel like a senator just walking up the steps. Senators, in particular, are fond of this feeling, and this is one reason official Washington escaped the worst effects of mod-ern architecture. Also, steel and glass skyscrapers are relatively cheap to build, and cost effectiveness is not a concept here.

—*Parliament of Whores* (1991)

Washington summertime tourists look only as Washington summertime tourists can: mature adults visiting their nation's most solemn monuments and greatest institutions in cartoon-character T-shirts and candy-colored running shoes the size of teddy bears, with porky desk-job thighs sticking out of tiny iridescent gym shorts and wearing fanny packs like phylacter-ies for the worship of fat.

—*Parliament of Whores* (1991)

WASTE

It is a popular delusion that the government wastes vast amounts of money through inefficiency and sloth. Enormous effort and elaborate planning are required to waste this much money.

—*Parliament of Whores* (1991)

WATER

Recall the national hullabaloo when icky stuff started to come out of the faucets in Flint, Michigan? We regard the ready availability of water—clean, pure water—as an inalienable human right. It's no such thing. Water doesn't come from the Declaration of Independence and the U.S. Constitution. Water comes from smart thinking and hard work.

—*None of My Business* (2018)

WEALTH

Lately there has been a lot of anger and indignation about wealth inequality. Some blame this on . . . wealth inequality. I blame it on rich people in T-shirts.

—*A Cry from the Far Middle* (2020)

It was just the usual small talk of the very rich, who are indeed different from you and me—they have tails. Little short ones with smooth silky hairs, right at the base of the spine. If you ever want to know whether somebody is very rich or not, just pull down their pants. If they're very rich, they'll have a tail. No kidding.

—*Age and Guile Beat Youth, Innocence, and a Bad Haircut* (1995)

Whenever we meet a rich person, however loathsome, we should be sure to say, "Thanks! The disgusting fact of your existence helps spread the manure of life around and keeps it from piling up in one spot, under the Capitol dome."

—*Don't Vote—It Just Encourages the Bastards* (2010)

WHAT THE COUNTRY NEEDS

What this country needs is fewer people who know what this country needs. We'd be better off, in my opinion, without so many opinions. Especially without so many political opinions.

—*A Cry from the Far Middle* (2020)

YANKEES

Yankees are serious about spending money. And they give advice at length on the subject. And they're especially forthcoming with advice about what you should have paid for your house. "You know that place sold for eight thousand in 1976."

—*Republican Party Reptile* (1987)

YOUNG PEOPLE

The early-seventies heroin craze petered out before emptying the nation's scout camps and Hi-Y chapters. And by the time PCP came along to make kids psychotic, kids were acting so psychotic anyway that who could tell the difference? The only unifying theme in these drug scares seemed to be an American public with a strong subconscious wish to be rid of its young people.

—*Parliament of Whores* (1991)

PART II

GOOD CLEAN FUN

It's better to spend money like there's no tomorrow than to spend tonight like there's no money.
—*Modern Manners* (1983)

There is only one basic human right, the right to do as you damn well please. And with it comes the only basic human duty, the duty to take the consequences.
—*Age and Guile Beat Youth, Innocence, and a Bad Haircut* (1995)

ALCOHOL

Alcohol makes you feel important when you are not. If you *are* important, it makes you feel safe. Alcohol gives you an incontrovertible reason not to have sexual relations. And, what's best, alcohol provides that most difficult of all things for an adult to achieve, sleep.

—*Modern Manners* (1983)

ARGUMENTS

Bluntness, especially when combined with obscenity or prejudice, can be very handy in arguments. It's rude to argue politics in public. Use strong language to take the politics out of your argument and make it personal again by saying to whoever disagrees with your position, "Fuck you."

—*Modern Manners* (1983)

BEING ON TIME

Whatever type of event you're attending, it's important to be on time. Being on time should not be confused with being prompt. Being prompt means arriving at the beginning. Being on time means arriving at the most interesting moment. Excepting love affairs, that moment is rarely the beginning.

—*Modern Manners* (1983)

BICYCLES

I don't like the kind of people who ride bicycles.

—Republican Party Reptile (1987)

BIG CARS

It's the bigness of the car that counts the most. Because when something bad happens in a big car—accidentally speeding through the middle of a gang of unruly young people who have been taunting you in a drive-in restaurant, for instance—it happens very far away, way out at the end of your fenders. It's like a civil war in Africa; it doesn't really concern you too much. On the other hand, when something happens in a little bitty car it happens right in your face. You get all involved in it and have to give everything a lot of thought.

—Driving Like Crazy (2009)

BOARD GAMES

Games, such as checkers, chess, and backgammon should always be played for money. Otherwise the stakes are psychological. You're betting you can humiliate someone and make him look like a fool. This is disgusting. No gentle person stoops to behavior like this unless he can make a buck at it.

—Modern Manners (1983)

BOXER SHORTS

It's not known why rich men wear boxer shorts, but it may be to show the world that they're too blasé to get sudden erections in public places or too rich and powerful to have to hide them.

—*Modern Manners* (1983)

CARS

Five hundred fifty-two horsepower in my control is like steak on a dinner plate.

—*Age and Guile Beat Youth, Innocence, and a Bad Haircut* (1995)

I love cars. But I love cars the way I love women. I don't know how to fix them. I wouldn't presume to design one. And, when they are beautiful and fast, they make me stupid enough to say such things as "I love cars the way I love women."

—*Age and Guile Beat Youth, Innocence, and a Bad Haircut* (1995)

There was no premarital sex in America before the invention of the internal combustion engine. You couldn't sneak a girl into the rec room of your house because your mom and dad were unable to commute so they were home all day working on the farm. And your farmhouse didn't have a rec room because recreation had not been discovered due to all the farm work. You could take a girl out in a buggy, but it was hard to get her in the mood to let you bust into her corset because the two of you were seated facing a horse rectum. It spoils the atmosphere.

—*Driving Like Crazy* (2009)

Oh, Jesus, that stupendous noise, that beautiful and astounding sound—not the flatulent blasting of the drag strip or the bucket-of-puppies squeal of tiny Grand Prix engines, but a full-bore iron-block stoked-out American symphony of monster pandemonium. Exhaust notes so low they shake the lungs like rubber bell clappers in the rib cage and shrieks of valves and gears and push rods wailing in the clear and terrifying soprano of the banshee's wail—I could not leave my ear plugs in, it was too beautiful.

—*Driving Like Crazy* (2009)

No matter how much the road surface resembled a pile of wet laundry, the Ferrari's tires stayed on it like spaghetti sauce stains. Acceleration was sufficient to leave earth orbit, and the brakes could stop time. On a two-lane road near Noplace, Maine, I came around an off-camber upchuck of a curve at ninety, and there, not a lunch toss away, was one logging truck overtaking another. The whole road and both shoulders were blocked by twenty thousand pounds of diesel and tree. I came through unscathed. I don't know how. The Ferrari did it. I closed my eyes.

—*Age and Guile Beat Youth, Innocence, and a Bad Haircut* (1995)

CHURCH

Church wouldn't seem to be a very interesting place to go. But that's not true. All sorts of perfectly normal activities— drinking, dope smoking, love-making—are somehow terrifically exciting when done in a church.

—*Modern Manners* (1983)

CIGARS

Giving really scarce, really good cigars to modish neophytes is like casting pearls before debutantes. They'll enjoy it, but I will not.

—*The CEO of the Sofa* (2001)

COCAINE

Cocaine is, *au fond*, the only truly polite drug. This is because cocaine makes us so intelligent, witty, charming, alert, well dressed, good looking, and sexually attractive. True, there are exceptions. Cocaine doesn't always do this to *you*. But cocaine always does this to the author.

—*Modern Manners* (1983)

If you buy your coffee at Starbucks, cocaine's probably cheaper.

—*The CEO of the Sofa* (2001)

COCAINE ETIQUETTE

The most important thing to understand about cocaine etiquette is that cocaine is bad for the health. And this is why it's never bad manners to go off alone and fire some "nose Nikes" and not share them with anyone else. To risk your own health while protecting the well-being of others is the only honorable thing to do. For the same reason, when offered someone else's cocaine, you should Electrolux as much as possible for their sake. They will be less inclined to destroy their mucous membranes, become psychotic, suffer heart palpitations, or die from an overdose if there isn't any left to take.

—*Modern Manners* (1983)

COCAINE ETIQUETTE QUESTIONS

Q. *How should cocaine be served?*

A. Nothing is more awkward than taking out a vial of "granulated money" in a bar or restaurant and having everyone you know expect to get some. If you try to pass the "powdered pole-vault" to some people and not to others, you may get slugged. And that's rude. Instead, excuse yourself inconspicuously, saying something like "Well, I sure have to go to the bathroom and so do Robert and Susan and Alice, but Jim and Fred and Bob don't have to go."

Q. *What should be served with cocaine?*

A. Most people enjoy a couple thousand cigarettes with their "face Drano." Others mix "indoor Aspen lift lines" with multiple sedatives to achieve that marvelous feeling so similar to not having taken drugs at all. But everyone, whether he wants to or not, should drink plenty of whiskey or gin. If you smell strongly of alcohol, people may think you are drunk instead of stupid.

Q. *Who pays?*

A. There's considerable debate about this. Some say the guest should pay for cocaine as a way of saying thank you to the host. Others say the host should pay for cocaine as part of the entertainment. Most people, however, say society at large should pay for cocaine by having to watch maniacally self-indulgent stand-up comedy routines, pathetically disconnected pop music performances, and dreadful late-night anti-drug commercials on television.

—*Modern Manners* (1983)

CRACK

Smoking crack is a way for people who couldn't afford college to study the works of Charles Darwin.

—*The CEO of the Sofa* (2001)

CREMATION

The ashes may be scattered over the food at the deceased's favorite restaurant, used in the litter box of his cats, or spread on the icy driveway of a friend's ski house in place of rock salt, which causes corrosion in automobiles and is harmful to plant-life ecology.

—*Modern Manners* (1983)

DEBUTANTES

A debutante party is basically a bar mitzvah with sex in the parking lot.

—*Modern Manners* (1983)

DEEP-SEA FISHING

Imagine a serious, highly competitive, physically demanding outdoor sport that you can play while sitting in a chair drinking beer. Deep-sea fishing is as close as a middle-aged man gets to heaven—unless he's not watching his cholesterol.

—*Age and Guile Beat Youth, Innocence, and a Bad Haircut* (1995)

There is, all told, a certain futility to deep-sea fishing. But it's a satisfying futility, like having sex with birth control.

—*Age and Guile Beat Youth, Innocence, and a Bad Haircut* (1995)

DINNER CONVERSATION

The better the wine, champagne, and brandy, the stronger and brighter the talk. Eschew the guest who doesn't drink. He's too likely to talk about why he doesn't. Also avoid hard liquor. The grape evokes the muses.

—*Republican Party Reptile* (1987)

The proper subject of dinner-table conversation with people other than best friends is savage criticism of the food. This used to be considered poor form, but that was when food was better and so were people.

—*Modern Manners* (1983)

In conversation, unlike bridge, it's bad taste to follow suit. If Miss A mentions that she knows an actress with 240 pairs of shoes, only a beast would let on that he's met a countess who owns three hundred. It is your duty as host to mitigate such trespasses. You have to say something to the effect of "Yes, the countess does own three hundred pairs of shoes. But her father was so impoverished by European tax laws that he was forced to marry a wealthy insect, and therefore the lady in question has six feet."

—*Republican Party Reptile* (1987)

Criticizing a hostess's food is now considered Christian charity compared to what you could be saying about the hostess herself.

—*Modern Manners* (1983)

DOGS

I'm a kind of god to my dog. When I say to my dog, "It shall be an abomination unto you to nose open the trash cabinet under the kitchen sink and eat garbage," what does my dog hear? *"Garbage!"*

—*How the Hell Did This Happen?* (2017)

Brittanys are very intelligent, whatever that means in a dog. Does a very intelligent dog have a unified theory of table scraps or a good and logical explanation for humping your leg?

—*Age and Guile Beat Youth, Innocence, and a Bad Haircut* (1995)

You speak to a child in the same tone of voice you speak to a dog, and you say almost the same things to both of them. "Good boy." "Down, boy." "Sit." All bachelors love dogs, and

we would love children just as much if they could be taught
to retrieve.

—The Bachelor Home Companion (1987)

DRINKING

I consider New Year's Eve to be the Special Olympics of
Inebriation.

—The CEO of the Sofa (2001)

When is it appropriate to get drunk? When you're sober.

—The CEO of the Sofa (2001)

Lushes are morally superior to uninebriated people.

—The CEO of the Sofa (2001)

If I stopped drinking and smoking, it would add ten years to
my life. But it would add them to the wrong end.

—The CEO of the Sofa (2001)

"I was drunk" is a better excuse than "I was stupid."

—The CEO of the Sofa (2001)

DRINKS

A Bloody Scotch is what you drink when you want a Bloody
Mary but don't have any vodka. It's just like a regular Bloody

Mary, but with Scotch instead of vodka, and without tomato juice, Worcestershire sauce, celery sticks, or any of the rest of that stuff. You drink it right out of the bottle.

—Age and Guile Beat Youth, Innocence, and a Bad Haircut (1995)

Alcohol's flavor is so bad that no one would ever drink an alcoholic beverage—unless, of course, it contained alcohol.

—The CEO of the Sofa (2001)

A mojito is made by mixing too much sugar with too much rum in not enough soda water and adding crushed mint leaves and lime juice. It sounds disgusting, and believe me, the next morning it is.

—Eat the Rich (1998)

DRIVING

I went around that hairpin before I could think. This didn't matter. I was in a realm beyond thought. I was transformed. A force, an inspiration flowed from the Bugatti's overbored 3.5-liter fuel-injected V-12 engine, through the throttle linkage, up my leg, and into this dull middle-aged corpus. My waist nipped in. My jowls grew taut. The lines in my bifocals disappeared. I had the acuity of a twenty-year-old, no, a ten-year-old tall enough to see over the dashboard. I had more skill, better coordination, and quicker reflexes than I'd ever possessed—than *anyone* had ever possessed.

—Age and Guile Beat Youth, Innocence, and a Bad Haircut (1995)

DRUGS

Every generation finds the drug it needs. The 1950s man, the corporate bevel gear, got silly on his dry martinis. The idiot hippie babbling in his pad had psychedelics to make it all mystic and smart. The wimps of the seventies took cocaine for their climb to the top. And the cold, selfish children of 1985 think Ecstasy will make them loved and loving. It's all pet food.

—*Republican Party Reptile* (1987)

Drugs are a one-man birthday party. You don't get any presents you didn't bring.

—*Republican Party Reptile* (1987)

I haven't taken a new drug in fifteen years. The mature adult—balanced, reasonable, facing the world and the self with a steady eye—doesn't need drugs. Except for one of those martinis every now and then or three or five of them and a line of blow if he's going out dancing later and some champagne and a joint and a fistful of Tylenol, Bloody Marys, Valium, and . . . what the hell, who's got the Ecstasy?

—*Republican Party Reptile* (1987)

Dope comes in just two dosages: too much and not enough.

—*Republican Party Reptile* (1987)

Drugs have caused a lot of people to do a lot of stupid things, such as hock their kid's Apple II, recite Rod McKuen poetry and stab Nancy Spungen.

—*Give War a Chance* (1992)

The problem with illicit drugs is that nobody knows anything about them—except for those of us who found out too much, and we have memory problems.

> —*The CEO of the Sofa* (2001)

If drugs turn out to be a case study showing that price has no connection with demand, every economics textbook will have to be rewritten. This will be an enormous bother if all the economists are stoned.

> —*The CEO of the Sofa* (2001)

Maybe drugs make you a better person but only if you believe in heaven and think John Belushi could get past the doorman.

> —*Age and Guile Beat Youth, Innocence,*
> *and a Bad Haircut* (1995)

I don't do drugs anymore. They interfere with the lithium, Viagra, and painkillers.

> —*The CEO of the Sofa* (2001)

DYING

If you must die, try to be considerate about it. Don't make antismoking commercials to be shown on TV after your death.

> —*Modern Manners* (1983)

If possible, die in a manner that entertains people while also impressing them with your attributes. Choking to death during autofellatio is an example.

—*Modern Manners* (1983)

If you're going to die in public, have something memorable ready to say:

"There's a million dollars buried in the yard right by the . . . by the . . . arrrrgh."

(Definitely memorable and good if the lawn needs to be dug up and reseeded.)

"Go fuck yourselves, the bunch of you."

(Trite, but will definitely be remembered by everyone present.)

—*Modern Manners* (1983)

Die young to create a livelier and more with-it funeral crowd.

—*Modern Manners* (1983)

ECSTASY

Ecstasy came in a largish plain pill. It was supposed to be stuff from the pre-illegal days but still looked, to this retired Aquarian, like it had been hand-made on a home tabbing machine. The dosage was . . . forget it. I recall long, lying discussions about mgs and mics in the days when I thought I had a Ph.D. in street pharmacology.

—*Republican Party Reptile* (1987)

THE EIGHTIES

Weren't the eighties grand? Cash grew on trees or, anyway, coca bushes. The rich roamed the land in vast herds hunted by proud, free tribes of investment brokers who lived a simple life in tune with money. Every wristwatch was a Rolex. Every car was a Mercedes-Benz. A fellow could romance a gal without shrink-wrapping his privates and negotiating the Treaty of Ghent. Communist dictators were losing their jobs, not presidents of America and General Motors. Women wore Adolfo gowns instead of dumpy federal circuit court judge robes. The Malcolm who mattered was Forbes. Bill Clinton was only a microscopic polyp in the colon of national politics, and Hillary was still in flight school, hadn't even soloed on her broom. What a blast we were having. The suburbs had just discovered Martha Stewart, the cities had just discovered crack. So many parties and none of them Democratic. Those were halcyon (and Valium and Lithium and Prozac) days. Think of all we owe to that glorious past. And the bank. Fin de fun.

—*The Bachelor Home Companion* (1993 foreword)

ENDURANCE SPORTS

Endurance sports provide people with the pain they seem to be missing from modern dentistry and health care.

—*Modern Manners* (1983)

ETIQUETTE

Every authority on etiquette discusses how to put things into your stomach, but very few discuss how to get them back out in a hurry.

—*Modern Manners* (1983)

The part of drinking where manners are really most involved is the part where you throw up.

—*Modern Manners* (1983)

The hallucinogenic drugs such as psilocybin, mescaline, and peyote are not rude *per se.* But it can be difficult to observe all the niceties of etiquette when you're being chased down the street by a nine-headed cactus demon.

—*Modern Manners* (1983)

EXERCISE

Exercise programs are the blue-collar equivalents of gambling. Instead of capitalism, they take the place of hard work. Hard work, of course, is always out of fashion.

—*Modern Manners* (1983)

FAMILY REVENGE

Elopement is a very unsatisfying method of getting revenge on your family for their objections to your marriage. It's much more spiteful to make them pay for an immense wedding reception even if you have to marry someone they like to get them to do it.

—*Modern Manners* (1983)

FERRARIS

Suppose you had 421 Budweiser Clydesdales trained to do anything you wanted, such as run through your boss's office or crash your ex-wife's dinner parties. The 512TR Ferrari is more fun than that.

—*Age and Guile Beat Youth, Innocence,*
and a Bad Haircut (1995)

FIRST CAR

From my first car I learned how, if you remove the hubcaps, reverse the tires so the whitewalls don't show, ventilate the muffler with an ice pick, replace the giant oil bath air cleaner with something cool in chrome, and pound aluminum spacers into the coil springs to jack up the front end . . . you'll still look like a dick in a 1956 four-door Ford Customline sedan your grandmother gave you. The more so if it's salmon pink.

—*The CEO of the Sofa* (2001)

FISHING

Fishing turns out to be less serene than it looks on calendars. It is a sport invented by insects and you are the bait.

—*Republican Party Reptile* (1987)

FLY-FISHING

When I began to think about fly-fishing, I realized I'd never be content again until my den was cluttered with computerized robot fly-tying vises, space-age Teflon and ceramic knotless tapered leaders, sterling silver English fish scissors, and thirty-five volumes on the home life of the midge. And there was one other thing. I'm a normal male who takes an occasional nip; therefore, I love to put funny things on my head. Sometimes it's the nut dish, sometimes the spaghetti colander, but the hats I'd seen fly fishermen wear were funnier than either and I had to have one.

—*Age and Guile Beat Youth, Innocence, and*
a Bad Haircut (1995)

Here's a guy standing in cold water up to his liver, throwing the world's most expensive clothesline at trees. A full two-thirds of his time is spent untangling stuff, which he could be doing in the comfort of his own home with old shoelaces, if he wanted. The whole business costs like sin and requires heavier clothing. Furthermore, it's conducted in the middle of blackfly season. Cast and swat. Cast and swat.

—*Age and Guile Beat Youth, Innocence, and*
a Bad Haircut (1995)

FORMAL DINNERS

Many people, when faced with a formal dinner, worry about what utensil to use and when. Although "using the right fork" is almost synonymous with "good etiquette," the phrase is largely symbolic. Among fashionable people this is not really considered very important. If your hostess happens to be as ignorant as you are and has laid out the silverware all wrong, then just use common sense. Put each implement to the use for which it seems most suited. Never stab anyone with a gravy ladle. And don't clean your ears with the fish knife. That should be done with the handle of the demitasse spoon. Also, don't steal silver that matches your own pattern at home. This looks too calculating. If all else fails, look around, watch what others are doing, and do the same thing. This should make for a delightful evening of drunkenness, flirtations, loud pointless laughter, and ill-advised invitations to your country place.

—*Modern Manners* (1983)

FRIENDS AND UNDERWEAR

Frequent changes of friends and underwear are marks of sophistication centuries old.

—*Modern Manners* (1983)

FRIENDS' DIVORCE

When you have been a mutual friend of the married couple and cannot decide where your allegiance lies, you should always side with the richer person. Given the mercenary nature of modern divorce lawyers, the richer person will, in the end, be the one more wronged.

—*Modern Manners* (1983)

FUN

"Having fun?" is a question posed only to those who clearly aren't.

—Holidays in Heck (2011)

Fun can be defined as "anything you don't have to do."
  —Age and Guile Beat Youth, Innocence, and a Bad Haircut (1995)

GAMBLING

Gambling is a replacement for entrepreneurial vigor and inventiveness. Entrepreneurial vigor and inventiveness are old-fashioned and don't leave time enough for the social graces. Thomas Edison and Henry Ford hardly ever got the chance to kick back on the waterbed, scarf some Chinese takeout, and listen to the new U2 album. They would have been a lot cooler heads if they'd made their money playing blackjack.

—Modern Manners (1983)

GARDENING

Vegetable gardening is frustrating. If anything does grow, the raccoons will take it and you'll have to call the Pentagon Rapid Deployment Force to get it back. What I do is just *say* I have a vegetable garden. I dig up some of the lawn, put on a raccoon suit, make tracks in the dirt, and go buy my vegetables at the local garden stand.

—Republican Party Reptile (1987)

GARDEN PARTIES

Garden parties consist of standing around in the garden. That's all. Sometimes sticky little drinks are served. The only way to get a worthwhile amount of alcohol out of these is to dunk your whole head in the punch bowl.

—*Modern Manners* (1983)

A GENTLEMAN'S CODE

1. Never strike anyone so old, small, or weak that verbal abuse would have sufficed.
2. Never steal anything so small that you'll have to go to an unpleasant city jail for it instead of a minimum security federal tennis prison.
3. Remember, the truth is rude. Consider the truth about where babies come from, especially some people's.
4. Never transmit a sexual disease in public.
5. Women and children should be protected in every tax-deductible way.
6. Don't pull on a crewneck sweater with a lit cigarette in your mouth.

—*Modern Manners* (1983)

GOING OUT

Going out is what you do when you don't have anything else to do. This is because modern people cannot stand to be by themselves for more than fifteen minutes. There is a strong contemporary aversion to bad company.

—*Modern Manners* (1983)

GOLF

Golf is so casual. You just go to the course, miss things, tramp around in the briars, use pungent language, and throw two thousand dollars' worth of equipment in a pond.

—*Age and Guile Beat Youth, Innocence, and a Bad Haircut* (1995)

Unlike skydiving or rugby, golf gives you leisure to realize it's pointless.

—*Age and Guile Beat Youth, Innocence, and a Bad Haircut* (1995)

There comes a time in life, however, when all the things that do have a point—career, marriage, exercising to stay fit—start turning, frankly, golf-like. And that's when you're ready for golf.

—*Age and Guile Beat Youth, Innocence, and a Bad Haircut* (1995)

Hitting things with a stick is the cornerstone of civilization. Consider all the things that can be improved by hitting them with a stick: veal, the TV, Woody Allen. Having a dozen good sticks at hand, all of them well balanced and expertly made, is one reason I took up golf.

—*Age and Guile Beat Youth, Innocence, and a Bad Haircut* (1995)

HORSEBACK RIDING

The term "horseback riding" covers a wide variety of athletic activities. All types of horseback riding, however, should be done on a horse. Doing them on a naked girl in a motel room is a different sport entirely, even if she lets you use spurs.

—*Modern Manners* (1983)

There are two principal types of riding in the United States: English and western. In English riding you don't have anything to hold on to and in western riding you do but they make fun of you if you use it. Don't wear chaps or carry a Winchester .30-30 when you ride English style, and don't wear a top hat and blow a French horn when riding western style. Don't wear a motorcycle helmet when you do either. It's a perfectly good idea, but it just isn't done.

—*Modern Manners* (1983)

HORSES VERSUS CARS

Horses are like your adolescent children. Cars are like your computer. The computer may be balky, slow, even worthless, but it never dresses itself all in black, gets every part of its keyboard pierced, screams that you just don't understand, and goes out and takes drugs and is brought home by the police at three in the morning. Actually, horses don't either. But you know what I mean.

—*Don't Vote—It Just Encourages the Bastards* (2010)

Cars, especially the cars of yore, were not reliable. But neither are horses, and at least with cars it isn't personal.

—*Don't Vote—It Just Encourages the Bastards* (2010)

HUNTING

Be sure to drink before hunting to give the animals a sporting chance to see some humans killed.

—*Modern Manners* (1983)

Hunting and fishing are the ways polite society gets the urge to murder out of its system. If your bloodlust is not being fully satisfied by these sports, maybe you should go a step further and pluck birds or gut deer *before* you kill them.

—*Modern Manners* (1983)

HUNTING (BIRDS)

I spend a lot of money every year and travel thousands of miles for my love of birds. I trudge across acres of muddy fields, push through tangles of forest underbrush, and hunker in swamps at dawn simply to find birds—and kill them. Call it tough love.

—*Holidays in Heck* (2011)

I regard it as armed shopping, a tame pursuit when you think about it. It's going to the grocery store that's bloodthirsty. Consider all those Perdue oven stuffers you've bought for dinner over the years. How many of them had any chance at all? You mighty nimrod, you. Every one you stalked you killed. Whereas for me, there's hardly a bird that comes before the barrels of my gun that doesn't get away free. Nay, better than free. The bird receives an education about what those orange and white and hairy—and pink and winded and pudgy—things are doing in the woods. I am a university for birds.

—*Age and Guile Beat Youth, Innocence, and a Bad Haircut* (1995)

HUNTING (DEER)

Deer hunting, particularly, attracts Visigothic types from places like Worcester, Massachusetts. I spend all of deer-hunting season indoors trying not to do anything deerlike.

—*Republican Party Reptile* (1987)

HUNTING (DUCKS)

The terrible thing about duck hunting is that everyone you're with can see you shoot and see what you're shooting at, and it is almost impossible to come up with a likely excuse for blasting a decoy in half.

—*Age and Guile Beat Youth, Innocence, and a Bad Haircut* (1995)

When you hunt you have to keep a careful eye on weather, terrain, foliage, and dangerous animals such as me if I happen to be in the cover with you swinging my gun around in every direction trying to get the safety to release. There's even a religious aspect to detailed examination of the outdoors. That said, alder patches [swampy duck-hunting terrain] are something God created on a Monday, after a big weekend.

—*Age and Guile Beat Youth, Innocence, and a Bad Haircut* (1995)

INFATUATION

The one serious dating pitfall is the possibility that the person you date may contract an infatuation for you. Infatuation is much more dangerous than love or marriage.

Modern marriages are happy, casual affairs, easily entered into and easily gotten out of. Modern love of one person for another is so rare that it hardly presents a problem. But now that love and marriage are no longer serious emotional concerns, infatuation is forced to bear the freight of all the human psyche's pathetic needs, drives, tensions, and energies. As a result, we have been turned into an entire society of fourteen-year-olds with crushes on our gym teacher. But, with the physical and financial freedoms of adulthood at our command, we are able to harass that gym teacher much more effectively than we could in junior high.

—Modern Manners (1983)

INSULTS

If you're skimming these pages in search of self-help tips, your mother dresses you funny.

—The Bachelor Home Companion (1993 foreword)

KEY WEST

I had fun there in the 1970s. At least I think I did. It's all blurry now. But I remember catching record-size hangovers in bars with three bathrooms: "Men," "Women," and "Drugs."

*—Age and Guile Beat Youth, Innocence, and
a Bad Haircut* (1995)

LITTERING

We Americans are long trained in highway citizenship. It's been thirty-five years since I threw something out a car window without guilt. I'd forgotten the pure exhilaration of littering and found myself heaving Coke cans and half-eaten sandwiches into the ether at every opportunity.

—Give War a Chance (1992)

LOS ANGELES

I stayed in Los Angeles for as long as I could stand it, which was four months (or, to put it in actress years, half a career).

—Driving Like Crazy (2009)

The Hollywooden heads buy a car for almost any purpose except a worthy one. Many automobiles are purchased to attract members of LA's eight or ten opposite sexes.

—Driving Like Crazy (2009)

LSD

LSD was supposed to make you think you could fly. I remember it made you think you couldn't stand up, and mostly it was right. The much-predicted heavy precipitation of wingless adolescents—which caused people to move their cars out from under trees near hippie pads—failed to materialize.

—Parliament of Whores (1991)

MANNERS

Good manners can replace intellect by providing a set of memorized responses to almost every situation in life. Memorized responses eliminate the need for thought. Thought is not a very worthwhile pastime anyway. Thinking allows the brain, an inert and mushy organ, to exert unfair domination over more sturdy and active body parts such as the muscles, the digestive system, and other parts of the body you can have a lot of thoughtless fun with.

—*Modern Manners* (1983)

MARIJUANA

Pot has become America's alternative brewski.

—*The CEO of the Sofa* (2001)

How much can you really say against a drug that makes teenage boys drive slow?

—*The CEO of the Sofa* (2001)

I can remember the antediluvian age of dope hysteria, when the occasional bebop musician's ownership of a Mary Jane cigarette threatened to turn every middle-class American teenager into a sex-crazed car thief. (This particular hysteria proved well-founded. Every middle-class American teenager did try marijuana and did become sex crazed—although no more car-thievish than usual.)

—*Parliament of Whores* (1991)

Medical marijuana is legal in forty-eight countries and in thirty-three U.S. states and all U.S. overseas territories. We know how it goes with medical marijuana. I have a great bumper sticker idea, yours free for the taking: "MEDICAL MARIJUANA MAKES ME SICK!"

—*A Cry from the Far Middle* (2020)

Weed is not going away, especially since weed is, in fact, a weed and grows like one.

—*The CEO of the Sofa* (2001)

MARTINIS

There is something in spirits distilled from grain that brings forth domestic animals. Gin martinis are particularly dangerous. Guests are reduced to dogs in their communicative abilities—sniffing and nipping at each other and raising the hair on the napes of their necks.

—*Republican Party Reptile* (1987)

MIND-ALTERING

I love that phrase, "mind-altering drugs." As if there were no changes in brain function after you drink six cups of coffee before doing your taxes or after you drink four martinis before putting the nut dish on your head, mounting the back of the sofa, and reciting "The Charge of the Light Brigade" to the cocktail party. But I digress. Which I find I'm doing a lot

while writing about the drug culture. It may have something
to do with the drugs. I'll have to go ask Alice, when she's ten
feet tall.

—*A Cry from the Far Middle* (2020)

MISBEHAVIOR

The first technique of misbehavior is to be cute. When the
generation born after World War II began to act up, they
wore feathers in their hair, put paint on their noses, and
went around sticking chrysanthemums down rifle barrels.
Life magazine adored it—it was so cute. But later they began
doing things which were much less cute, like threatening to
vote, and it became necessary to kill them at Kent State. Of
course, hippies were also violating a basic principle of cuteness; they were getting old. To be cute you must be young. If
you had a great big adult dog and it whined all night, tore up
your shoes, and messed on the rug, you'd have it gassed. But
when a puppy does these things, it's cute.

—*Modern Manners* (1983)

MOTORCYCLES

It's hard to drink while you're riding a motorcycle—there's
no place to set your glass. And cocaine's out of the question.
And personally, I find that pot makes me too sensitive. You
smoke some pot and the first thing you know you're pulling
over to the side of the road and taking a break to dig the gentle
beauty of the sky's vast panorama, the slow, luxurious interplay

of sun and clouds, the lulling trill of breezes midst leafy tree branches—and what kind of fun is that?

—Driving Like Crazy (2009)

It's tough to "get it on" with a chick (I mean in the biblical sense) and still make all the fast curves unless you let her take the handlebars with her pants off and come on doggy style or something, which is harder than it sounds.

—Driving Like Crazy (2009)

ORAL SEX

Oral sex is currently very trendy. It is even preferred to the regular kind. It is preferred because it's the only way most of us can get our sex partners to shut up.

—Modern Manners (1983)

A few rules of common courtesy should be observed during oral sex: Never do anything to your partner with your teeth that you wouldn't do to an expensive waterproof wristwatch.

—Modern Manners (1983)

PARTIES

There is only one hard-and-fast rule about the place to have a party: someone else's place.

—Modern Manners (1983)

PICKUP TRUCKS

An experienced pickup truck driver is a person who's wrecked one. An inexperienced pickup truck driver is a person who's about to wreck one.

—*Republican Party Reptile* (1987)

A pickup truck is basically a back porch with an engine attached. Both a pickup and a back porch are good places to drink beer because you can take a leak standing up from either. Pickup trucks are generally a little faster downhill than back porches, with the exception of certain California back porches during mudslide season.

—*Republican Party Reptile* (1987)

Today's pickup trucks are full-size four-door luxury sedans except as tall as a house and with doorsills so high that you have to stand on a Prius to get inside. What are these pickup truck drivers picking up? The pickup beds are the size of a backyard aboveground pool and there's never anything in them. Yet, in the next lane over, there will be a Fiat 500 with a mattress and a box spring bungee-corded to the roof, a back seat full of moving cartons and kitchen appliances, and a sectional couch hanging out of the hatchback. Do we need to introduce these folks to each other?

—*A Cry from the Far Middle* (2020)

PLAYING WITH FOOD

- Playing with food is the main reason that dining in restaurants has become so popular.

- Playing with food is a psychologically powerful way of attracting attention to yourself.
- And restaurants are better places to attract attention than friends' homes are, anyway.
- You usually know who's going to be at a friend's home. But practically anybody could be at a restaurant.
- If you attract enough attention in a restaurant, maybe a rich, beautiful person will give you money and sex.
- Playing with food is easy. There are so many wonderful props right at hand. Breathes there a man with soul so dead that he's immune to the theatrical possibilities of a plate full of fried calamari?

—*Modern Manners* (1983)

POLO

I once thought polo was nothing more than a punch line for jokes about rich people. Then, thirty years ago, I saw my first polo match. It's an amazing sport, a combination of rodeo trick riding, mounted golf, horse soccer, rugby on four legs, and the Super Bowl played with thousand-pound running backs.

—*None of My Business* (2018)

PRIVATE LIFE

What we do in our private lives is private. We can take all the drugs we like as long as we don't admit to it publicly.

—*The CEO of the Sofa* (2001)

RENTAL CARS

There's a lot of debate about what kind of car handles best.
Some say a front-engined car; some say a rear-engined car. I
say a *rented* car. You can go faster, turn corners sharper, and
put the transmission into reverse while going forward at a
higher rate of speed in a rented car than in any other kind.
You can also park without looking, and you can use the trunk
as an ice chest. A rented car is an all-terrain vehicle. Mud,
snow, water, woods—you can take a rented car anywhere.
True, you can't always get it back—but that's not your problem, is it?

—Republican Party Reptile (1987)

RUNNING

If you run more than twenty miles a week, try not to die young.
It will make people snigger.

—Modern Manners (1983)

SALAD

Salad is so seventies, like platform shoes and disco.

—The Bachelor Home Companion (1987)

Any lettuce that comes from the store in a form that can't
be thrown from third base to home is too exotic.

—The Bachelor Home Companion (1987)

SALT

Salt keeps your blood pressure up to the pitch of modern life and improves all foods. Without salt, pretzels would be nothing but breadsticks with bad posture and potato chips would be potatoes. Use salt in everything.

—*The Bachelor Home Companion* (1987)

SEX

Sexual experimentation and even perversion have gained a sort of general social acceptance like using the same size glasses for red and white wine.

—*Modern Manners* (1983)

There are a number of mechanical devices which increase sexual arousal, particularly in women. Chief among these is the Porsche 911 Cabriolet.

—*Modern Manners* (1983)

Emotional bonds have also come to the fore as a metaphysical raison d'être, as has hedonistic pleasure seeking. Liver trouble and bad breath have been advanced as virtually airtight refutations of such romantic and neo-Epicurean arguments. As Bertrand Russell points out in *Principia Mathematica*, "Fucking would be all right except women smell bad and slobber." Edna St. Vincent Millay has noted the same characteristics in other sexes.

—*Age and Guile Beat Youth, Innocence, and a Bad Haircut* (1995)

SINKING SHIPS

If you happen to be on a sinking ship with too few lifeboats, take one and slip quietly away. There's going to be a terrific fuss among the drowning passengers, and it's rude to deliberately overhear an argument which is none of your concern.

—*Modern Manners* (1983)

THE SIXTIES

The 1960s was an era of large thoughts. And yet, amazingly, each of those thoughts could fit on a T-shirt.

—*The Baby Boom* (2014)

"If you can remember the sixties you weren't there" is a quote variously attributed to Grace Slick, Dennis Hopper, Robin Williams, and a bunch of other people because—you guessed it—nobody from back then can remember anything.

—*A Cry from the Far Middle* (2020)

Maybe we should freshen our recollections a bit. About drugs. We're only remembering the cool ones like marijuana, LSD (if you didn't have to talk to your folks on it), and psilocybin mushrooms. What about the STP, the PCP, the Thorazine, the crystal meth, and the little blue-green tab somebody laid on you in the park and you vomited so hard your socks came out your mouth?

—*Age and Guile Beat Youth, Innocence, and a Bad Haircut* (1995)

The mood police came. Your face had to go to jail. Not everybody can turn his toes into ten angry, hissing lizards with rows
and rows of sharp little teeth. Quick! Help! Grab that chick,
she just swallowed her superego. She could mellow to death
at any moment. Ha, ha, ha, somebody left the lava lamp on all
night and now the entire island of Oahu is gone. Wow, man,
which way to the bummer tent?

—*Age and Guile Beat Youth, Innocence, and a Bad Haircut* (1995)

Marxism is a perfect example of the chimeras that fueled the
sixties. And it was probably the most potent one. Albeit, much
of this Marxism would have been unrecognizable to Marx.
It was Marxism watered down, Marxism spiked with LSD and
Marxism adulterated with mystical food coloring. But it was
Marxism nonetheless because the wildest hippie and the stern-
est member of the Politburo shared the same daydream, the
daydream that underlies all Marxism: *that a thing might somehow
be worth other than what people will give for it.*

—*Give War a Chance* (1992)

I've thought about this. I'm pretty sure, during the entire 1960s,
I never once linked a subject to a predicate with a verb to create
a sentence that meant anything. No wonder we were so interested in talking to dolphins. We sure couldn't talk to each other.

—*Age and Guile Beat Youth, Innocence, and a Bad Haircut* (1995)

SKIING

The sport of skiing consists of wearing three thousand dollars'
worth of clothes and equipment and driving two hundred

miles in the snow in order to stand around at a bar and get drunk.

—*Modern Manners* (1983)

SKYDIVING

The only polite thing to do when engaged in sky diving, hang gliding, ice climbing, or any other dangerous sport is die. That's what everyone's waiting around for.

—*Modern Manners* (1983)

SOBRIETY

There are times when it would be really bad manners to be sober. Some of these occasions are:

- Funeral of anyone you knew or claimed to
- Daughter's wedding reception
- Own wedding
- Anytime the Dow-Jones average drops more than 500 points in a day

Not to be drunk in these situations will make you look unfeeling, insensitive, and in the case of the last, financially inconsequential.

—*Modern Manners* (1983)

Hitler was a teetotaler.

—*The CEO of the Sofa* (2001)

SOFTBALL

There is nothing to say about softball as a sport. No one has ever paid enough attention either while watching or playing to be able to remember anything about it.

—Modern Manners (1983)

SO HIGH DID YOU GET?

Man, I come from the days when drugs were drugs. We had dope where one toke would turn your hair long and your folks into raving maniacs at the dinner table. Some of that stuff, why, a single hit could transform a Catholic schoolgirl into Gomorrah on all fours, snuff your ego like a light, rotate the tires on the Great Wheel of Being, and make your eyes lay eggs. See God? Shit, you could get Him down in the hot tub and wash His mouth out with herbal soap. And that was if you split the blotter paper four ways. As for insights, try yage and psilocybin mushrooms mixed with mescaline and Anchor Steam beer. Gautama Buddha his own bad self comes over to your house and writes out the Eightfold Path in lipstick on your bathroom mirror. We had drugs that would give you immortal life for up to thirty-six hours. And what about the time the nine-assed peyote demon peeled the top of my head like an orange and vomited the *Encyclopaedia Britannica* into my empty skull? That's what we meant when we said *high* in the old days.

—Republican Party Reptile (1987)

SPEED

There is no more profound feeling of control over one's destiny than to drive a Ferrari down a public road at 130 miles an hour. Only God can make a tree, but only man can drive by one that fast.

—*Republican Party Reptile* (1987)

A 930 Turbo Porsche was going about ninety when we passed him in the Ferrari, and he gave us a little bit of a run, passed us at about 110, and then we passed him again. He was as game as anybody we came across and was hanging right on our tail at 120. Ah, but then—then we just *walked* away from him. Five seconds and he was nothing but a bathtub-shaped dot in the mirrors. I suppose he could have kept up, but driving one of those ass-engined Nazi slot cars must be a task at around 225 percent of the speed limit. But not for us. I've got more vibration here on my electric typewriter than we had blasting into Birmingham that beautiful morning in that beautiful car on a beautiful tour across this wonderful country from the towers of Manhattan to the bluffs of Topanga Canyon so fast we filled the appointment logs of optometrists' offices in thirty cities just from people getting their eyes checked for seeing streaks because they'd watched us go by.

—*Republican Party Reptile* (1987)

SPORTS

Some sports, such as croquet, pool, badminton, and touch football, are actually a lot of fun to play. Unfortunately, playing sports for fun is quite out of fashion at the moment. Perhaps this is because modern people are doing so many other things—divorcing, developing drug habits, screwing up their children—for fun. In order to make fun sports socially acceptable, they must be played in deadly earnest and practiced in secret and argued over loudly.

—*Modern Manners* (1983)

SUBURBANS

Let's blast through a crafts fair (the Suburban has 210 horsepower so it won't get snagged in any macramé) and drive into the middle of one of those men's liberation inner-warrior weekends and chase flabby guys in loincloths out of the woods.

—*Age and Guile Beat Youth, Innocence, and a Bad Haircut* (1995)

TABLE MANNERS

The table manners you have in a restaurant are very different from those you have in the home of a friend because, in a restaurant, you're allowed to play with your food. If you eat enough expensive meals and drink enough expensive liquor in a restaurant, you're allowed to do anything. But in the home of a friend, no matter how much you eat and drink, it won't excuse you for "restoring" a Renoir with potatoes *au gratin.*

—*Modern Manners* (1983)

TALKING WITH YOUR MOUTH FULL

Talking with the mouth full is all right. Everyone does it. But don't listen with the mouth empty. It looks too much as though you're paying close attention to what's being said. And if you do that, people won't say things they really shouldn't.

—*Modern Manners* (1983)

TENNIS

Tennis players aren't stodgy anymore, but tennis fans are still real stick-in-the-muds. Show them how to have a good time the way college football fans do. Bring a TV and a gallon of martinis into the stands and make up loud cheers:

> *Throw that racket!*
> *Swear out loud!*
> *Slap the ball boy!*
> *Moon the crowd!*
> *ENDORSEMENTS! ENDORSEMENTS! ENDORSEMENTS!*

—*Modern Manners* (1983)

TRAVEL

There's no reason to behave any differently from normal when you travel. In fact, there's no reason to behave at all. You're never going to see these people again, so what do you care?

—*Modern Manners* (1983)

TUXEDOS AND WOMEN

The two most rented-looking things in the world are a rented woman and a rented tuxedo.

—Modern Manners (1983)

VICE

A shared vice is a pleasure.

—The CEO of the Sofa (2001)

VIDEO GAMES

There is something about a television that fights back which is so perfectly appropriate to our society.

—Modern Manners (1983)

WEDDING RECEPTIONS

Wedding receptions differ according to types of excess, the type of excess being determined by religious affiliation. There is an excess of relatives at a Catholic wedding, an excess of food at a Jewish wedding, and an excess of station wagons at a Protestant wedding so that people have to park all over the grass.

—Modern Manners (1983)

Wedding-reception food, whether served at tables or presented at a buffet, should be stuff that's easy to throw up, like spaghetti.

—*Modern Manners* (1983)

The first toast to the bride should come from the best man, who is expected to avoid complimenting her on her skill in bed, at least in so many words. Toasts should go on until the men have to go to the locker room and get the Scotch bottles out of their golf bags. Do not throw the glasses into the fireplace if it's more than forty feet away.

—*Modern Manners* (1983)

If the groom is a military officer, the cake is traditionally cut with his dress sword. However, if the groom is an arbitrage specialist or trader in the junk bond market, no attempt should be made to cut the cake with a subpoena.

—*Modern Manners* (1983)

WEEKENDS

Everybody should have a day of rest. This doesn't have to be a religious thing, although many sensible religions require it. The Muslims say Friday. The Jews say Saturday. The Christians say Sunday. I say "Three-Day Weekend!"

—*None of My Business* (2018)

WINE

I'm one of those people who, as I've mentioned before, can't figure out why wine-tasting columns don't mention getting drunk. That *is* the point.

—*The CEO of the Sofa* (2001)

Never refuse wine. It is an odd but universally held opinion that anyone who doesn't drink must be an alcoholic.

—*Modern Manners* (1983)

I'm careful with things like stairs and go down to the wine cellar only four times on any given evening.

—*Don't Vote—It Just Encourages the Bastards* (2010)

YACHTING

If a yacht is too expensive, you can get the same effect in your living room with strobe lights and milk punch.

—*The Bachelor Home Companion* (1987)

PART III

AROUND THE WORLD

I thought maybe I could use the techniques of humor to report on real news events. Or, at least, I thought I could use that phrase to convince editors and publishers to pay my way to Lebanon, El Salvador and so forth. Actually, I was just curious. I wanted to know where trouble came from and why the world was such a lousy place. I wasn't curious about natural disasters—earthquakes, mudslides, floods and droughts. These are nothing but the losing side of the Grand Canyon coin toss. Okay, it's sad. Now what? I was curious about the trouble man causes himself and which he could presumably quit causing himself at the drop of a hat, or, anyway, a gun. I wanted to know why life, which ought to be an only moderately miserable thing, is such a frightful, disgusting, horrid thing for so many people in so many places.

—*Holidays in Hell* (1988)

AIRPORTS

Airport security would soon be turned over to the government so that a federal agency could do the same fine job of protecting the nation in the future that the CIA and the FBI did in early September. Meanwhile "heightened security precautions" were allowing airlines to perfect their technique of treating passengers like convicted felons and providing all the transportation amenities usually accorded to smuggled cockatoos.

—*Peace Kills* (2004)

ALBANIA

All of Albania's rich and varied manifestations of freedom . . . came to a halt promptly at 10 P.M., when the shoot-to-kill curfew began.

—*Eat the Rich* (1998)

There was an Albanian family at the next table: handsome young husband, pretty wife, baby in a stroller, cute four-year-old girl bouncing on her dad's knee. The girl grabbed the cigarette from between her father's lips and tried a puff. Mom and Dad laughed. Dad took the cigarette back. Then he pulled a pack of Marlboros from his shirt pocket, offered a fresh cigarette to the little girl, and gave her a light.

—*Eat the Rich* (1998)

The population of Albania was 3.2 million. And, as far as I was able to tell, all of them had invested in pyramid schemes. . . . The [secret was that] Albanians didn't believe they were victims of a scam. They believed they were the perpetrators.

—*None of My Business* (2018)

AMERICAN FOREIGN AID

A hundred years ago when foreign aid was unthought of (except as tribute or bribe) we were a respected and admired country. After a century of philanthropy everyone hates our guts.

—*Don't Vote—It Just Encourages the Bastards* (2010)

AMERICAN INFLUENCE

All around the world people are imitating America—wearing blue jeans, listening to rock and roll and rap, tweeting, posting on Facebook, playing violent video games, binge-watching *Crazy Ex-Girlfriend*, eating junk food, and becoming obese. We should be getting royalties for this.

—*How the Hell Did This Happen?* (2017)

BMI and ASCAP have made the royalty model work for American popular music. Since "White Christmas" was copyrighted by Irving Berlin in 1940, it has earned $36 million in worldwide royalties. Imagine each American getting even a few pennies in licensing fees from 7.4 billion people every time any one of

those people wears an ugly T-shirt, says "OK," or burns off his
eyebrows lighting the BBQ grill.

—*How the Hell Did This Happen?* (2017)

ARABS

One by one and man to man Arabs are the salt of the earth—
generous, hospitable, brave, wise, and so forth. But get them
in a pack and shove a Koran down their pants and they act
like a footlocker full of glue-sniffing civet cats.

—*Holidays in Hell* (1988)

Arab table manners are the best in the world or, anyway, the
most fun.

—*Holidays in Hell* (1988)

ASIA

Civilization was born in Asia some nine thousand years ago.
This means the people of Asia have—give or take—nine thousand more years of being civilized than we do. I have never
spoken intimately to a person from Asia who did not consider
Westerners to be barbarians. And it's true. The World War II
that the world had not long ago was based entirely on Western
ideologies (including the fascism of Imperial Japan), and the
worst tragedy that has befallen modern Asia—the gruesome
depredations of Maoism—was also based on a Western ideology. We are guilty as charged.

—*None of My Business* (2018)

AUSTRALIA

Australia is not very exclusive. On the visa application they still ask if you've been convicted of a felony—although they are willing to give you a visa even if you haven't been.

—*Holidays in Hell* (1988)

We pushed on through misty, too-lush monkeypod forests and out into pastures greener than a rich Protestant's go-to-hell pants.

—*Age and Guile Beat Youth, Innocence,*
and a Bad Haircut (1995)

Not many people live here, and I'm not so sure about those who do. Every time I got out of a car to relieve myself, the sheep would start backing toward me, looking over their shoulders expectantly.

—*Age and Guile Beat Youth, Innocence,*
and a Bad Haircut (1995)

I never saw a kangaroo. I saw kangaroo posters and kangaroo postcards and thousands of kangaroo T-shirts. Kangaroos appear on practically every advertising logo and trademark. You can buy kangaroo-brand oleo and kangaroo bath soap, and get welcome mats, shower curtains, and beach towels with kangaroos on them and have kangaroos all over your underpants. But as for real live kangaroos, I think they're all in the Bronx Zoo.

—*Holidays in Hell* (1988)

AUSTRALIAN TOURISTS

At least we American tourists understand English when it's spoken loudly and clearly enough. Australians don't. Once you've been on a plane full of drunken Australians doing wallaby imitations up and down the aisles, you'll never make fun of Americans visiting the Wailing Wall in short shorts again.

—*Holidays in Hell* (1988)

BAJA

Ah, the sights, the smells, the vistas, the stronger smells, and the wonderful, beautiful weather. The weather in Baja is incomparable, glorious year-round. Don't call it rain, call it liquid sunshine. Why, the climate is so warm and dry that the Mexicans don't even bother to build bridges. They just pave right across the bottom of arid river beds and never have any problems at all with . . . WHERE'S SHERMAN? JESUS CHRIST, GET ROPE! GET SANDBAGS! Happy touring, *amigos*, and *adiós* for now to the cheerful, fun-filled . . . BAIL, FOR GOD'S SAKE! BAIL! MAYDAY! MAY-DAY! MAYDAY!

—*Driving Like Crazy* (2009)

BOMBING

Wherever there's suffering, injustice, and oppression, America will show up six months late and bomb the country next to where it's happening.

—*Peace Kills* (2004)

CANADA

If Canada's health care is so great, how come more Americans aren't apprehended at the border trying to sneak into Ontario to get free liposuction? Such comparisons are of limited value anyway. Canada is a sparsely populated nation with a shortage of gunshot wounds, crack addicts, and huge tort judgments. What can we really learn from a medical system devoted to hockey injuries and sinus infections caused by trying to pronounce French vowels?

—*Age and Guile Beat Youth, Innocence, and a Bad Haircut* (1995)

CHECKPOINTS

The Druse militiamen were good-natured. "Do you speak Arabic?" asked one. I shook my head, and he said something to another soldier who poked face and gun into the car and shouted, "He just said he wants to fuck your mother!" At least, I assume this was good-natured.

—*Holidays in Hell* (1988)

I was stopped at a checkpoint manned—or I should say boyed—by fifteen- and sixteen-year-old members of the militant Islamic fundamentalist Hezbollah. One of the young militants pointed his AK-47 at my face. He demanded my passport. When he saw that I was an American he subjected me to a twenty-minute tirade, at gunpoint, about America Satan Devil and how the United States had caused the Lebanese civil war, colonialism, imperialism, Zionism, and every other problem he could think of. Then he handed my passport back and said, "As soon as I get my green card I am going to dentist school in Dearborn, Michigan."

—*The Baby Boom* (2014)

The interesting thing about staring down a gun barrel is how small the hole is where the bullet comes out, yet what a big difference it would make in your social schedule. Not that people shoot you very often, but the way they flip those weapons around and bang them on the pavement and poke them in the dirt and scratch their ears with the muzzle sights. . . . Gun safety merit badges must go begging in the Lebanese Boy Scouts.

—*Holidays in Hell* (1988)

CHINA

A system such as China's, which allows citizens to trade in most physical objects but forbids them to trade in certain intellectual concepts, is like a system where everybody gets a car but nobody is allowed to learn to drive. Sooner or later there's going to be a crack-up.

—*None of My Business* (2018)

If our wonks are going to worry, they should worry about China. The Chinese have—let us not forget Tiananmen Square— worse politics than we do. If China can't keep its economic progress going, the political consequences could be dire. Gang of Four: The Adventure Continues. Great Leap Backward.

—*Don't Vote—It Just Encourages the Bastards* (2010)

THE CIA

A missile hit the Souq Sharq. The Kuwaitis claimed it was a
"Seersucker" missile. Who names these things, leftover old
preppies at the CIA? Next, we'll have the Madras Cummer-
bund missile and the Lime Green Pants with Little Trout Flies
missile.

—*Peace Kills* (2004)

COBRA BLOOD

There's a ritual involved in drinking cobra blood. Of
course. There's a ritual involved in most very silly things.
You have to get four males together and pledge a toast or
something, and something else, which I don't remember. Do
I need to mention we were drunk? Then you slam it.

Being that a snake is a "cold-blooded" animal, I vaguely expected
a chilled beverage. But it turns out a snake is a room-temperature
animal. Which allows the full flavor to come through.

Drinking cobra blood makes you . . . it's very good for . . .
gives you lots of . . . The explanation was in Chinese. And
cobra gallbladder juices do whatever even more. We let the
youngest guy drink this. He said it was okay, although he was
awake all night chasing mice around his hotel room.

—*Eat the Rich* (1998)

THE COLD WAR

The tic-tac-toe of Cold War diplomacy has given way to the foreign policy conundrums of tri-dimensional chess, like Captain

Kirk and Mr. Spock played on the starship *Enterprise,* except the pawns have nukes.

—*Parliament of Whores* (1991)

COMMUNISM

It's impossible to get decent Chinese takeout in China, Cuban cigars are rationed in Cuba, and that's all you need to know about communism.

—*Give War a Chance* (1992)

For all the meddling the Communist bloc countries have done in banana republics, they still never seem to be able to get their hands on any actual bananas.

—*Give War a Chance* (1992)

The Chinese Communists are attempting to build capitalism from the top down, as if the ancient Egyptians had constructed the Pyramid of Khufu by saying, "Thutnefer, you hold up this two-ton pointy piece while the rest of the slaves go get 2,300,000 blocks of stone."

—*Eat the Rich* (1998)

Nobody hates a commie worse than me. When they were negotiating, their demands were straight out of the Mickey Maoist Club bylaws. They are red as a baboon's ass, and that means freeze-and-assume-the-position as far as I'm concerned. I've been to your communist countries. They are crap-your-pants-ugly, dull-as-church, dead-from-the-dick-up places where government is to life what panty hose are to sex.

—*Holidays in Hell* (1988)

CUBA

I was in constant danger of being serenaded.

—*Eat the Rich* (1998)

If you were designing a socialist system—a nation in which everyone had the same social status—wouldn't eliminating restroom attendants be the first thing you'd do? And if I were designing a socialist system (what a hobby), I'd at least let the masses visit the hotel that they all supposedly own in common. But ordinary Cubans can't enter the Nacional or its several acres of seaside gardens unless they are, for instance, rest-room attendants.

—*Eat the Rich* (1998)

Some people were walking dogs. All the dogs were old and small, the kind kept by rich women for purposes of baby talk. Maybe the dogs had been left behind when the rich women fled the revolution—thirty-seven-year-old miniature schnauzers forced to pawn their costume-jewelry collars and have their fur clipped at barber colleges.

—*Eat the Rich* (1998)

Cuban nationalization does to goods and services what divorce does to male parents—suddenly they're absent most of the time and useless the rest.

—*Eat the Rich* (1998)

You have to watch out when you drive in Cuba, but you never know what you're watching out for.

—*Eat the Rich* (1998)

Much work had been done painting propaganda slogans. SOCIALISM OR DEATH appeared on almost every overpass. What if the U.S. government had slogans all over the place? I tried to come up with a viable campaign. My suggestion, AMERICA—IT DOESN'T SUCK.

—*Eat the Rich* (1998)

EARTH DAY

Contempt for material progress is not only unfair but dangerous. The average Juan and the average Chang and the average Mobutu out there in the parts of the world where every day is Earth Day, or Dirt and Squalor Day would like to have a color television, too. He'd also like some comfy Reeboks and a Nintendo Power Glove and a Jeep Cherokee. And he means to get them. I wouldn't care to be the skinny health-food nut waving a copy of *Fifty Simple Things You Can Do to Save the Earth* who tries to stand in Juan's way.

—*Parliament of Whores* (1991)

EAST GERMANY

East Germany was so total in its totalitarianism that everything
was banned which wasn't compulsory.

—*Give War a Chance* (1992)

How the Commies managed to make a poor country out of
a nation full of Germans is a mystery.

—*Give War a Chance* (1992)

EGYPT

A certain amount of craziness can be acquired trying to walk
in Cairo. The city is well supplied with sidewalks, but they just
take you around the block. You can't step off them because of
the traffic. I began thinking that Cairenes employ some chapter of the ancient Egyptian Book of the Dead, which I missed
when I was a hippie, that tells them how to keep going after
they've been squashed between two trucks.

—*Peace Kills* (2004)

ELEPHANTS

Elephants leave a real mess in the woods. They leave a mess
wherever they go. You can see how in a country supported by
humble agricultural endeavors, the big browsing animals get
killed. And not just by poachers. We love elephants in North
America, where they never get into our tomato plants or

herbaceous borders, much less destroy the equivalent of our fax machines and desktop computers.

—*Eat the Rich* (1998)

EL SALVADOR

El Salvador has the scenery of northern California and the climate of southern California plus—and this was a relief—no Californians.

—*Holidays in Hell* (1988)

EMBASSIES

American embassies are all over the map and always breathtaking. In the middle of London, on beautiful Grosvenor Square, there's one that looks like a bronzed Oldsmobile dashboard. And rising from the slums of Manila is another that resembles the Margarine of the Future Pavilion at the 1959 Brussels World Fair. I assume this is all the work of one architect, and I assume he's on drugs.

—*Holidays in Hell* (1988)

Each American embassy comes with two permanent features—a giant anti-American demonstration and a giant line for American visas. Most demonstrators spend half their time burning Old Glory and the other half waiting for green cards.

—*Holidays in Hell* (1988)

ENGLAND

Oxford and Cambridge have courses in anthropology, sociology, psychology, political science, economics, and no telling what else. Meanwhile the British Empire has shrunk to three IRA informants, a time-share deal with the Red Chinese in Hong Kong, and that bed-and-breakfast of an island, Bermuda. *Sic transit gloria mundi*, as if anybody knew what that meant anymore.

—*Age and Guile Beat Youth, Innocence, and
a Bad Haircut* (1995)

There is a nice hill where Saint George slew the dragon. (Unanswered questions: Was it dragon season? Is it sporting to slay them when they aren't on the wing? Was Saint George careful to extinguish all dragon-breath fires and pick up the spent lance tips and empty mead cans in his dragon blind?) No grass will grow on the place where the dragon's blood was spilled. This is because people walk around on it all the time, looking for the place where grass won't grow.

—*Age and Guile Beat Youth, Innocence, and
a Bad Haircut* (1995)

THE ENGLISH LANGUAGE

Foreigners may pretend otherwise, but if English is spoken loudly enough, anyone can understand it, the British included.
—*Modern Manners* (1983)

One of the pleasures of going someplace where people don't speak English is making fun of the English the people don't speak there.

—*Give War a Chance* (1992)

ETHIOPIA

A jolly soldier rummaged through my carry-on baggage, airily dismissing my pocketknife as a possible weapon and telling me that the woman operating the metal detector was his sister and would love to go along. I was ushered into the "boarding lounge" for the requisite two- or three-hour wait before anything airplane-like happens in Tanzania. Warm soft drinks were for sale by a young lady with no change.

—*Eat the Rich* (1998)

EUROPE

Everything in Europe is lukewarm except the radiators. You could use the radiators to make party ice. But nobody does. I'll bet you could walk from the Ural Mountains to the beach at Biarritz and not find one rock-hard, crystal-clear, fist-sized American ice cube. Ask for whiskey on the rocks, and you get a single, gray, crumbling leftover from some Lilliputian puddle freeze plopped in a thimble of Scotch (for which you're charged like sin). And the phones don't work. They go "blat-blat" and "neek-neek" and "ugu-ugu-ugu." No two dial tones are alike. The busy signal sounds as if the phone is ringing. And when the phone rings you think the dog farted.

—*Holidays in Hell* (1988)

The Europeans can't figure out which side of the road to drive on, and I can't figure out how to flush their toilets.

—Holidays in Hell (1988)

I've had it with these dopey little countries and all their poky borders. You can't swing a cat without sending it through customs. Everything's too small. The cars are too small. The beds are too small. The elevators are the size of broom closets. Even the languages are itty-bitty. Sometimes you need two or three just to get you through till lunch.

—Holidays in Hell (1988)

FAMINE

Famine is too close to dieting. We snap at our spouses, jiggle on the scale, and finish other people's cheesecake. If we're turned into angry, lying thieves by a mere forgoing of dessert, what must real hunger be like? Imagine a weight-loss program at the end of which, instead of better health, good looks and hot romantic prospects, you die.

—All the Trouble in the World (1994)

FRANCE

The French are a smallish, monkey-looking bunch and not dressed any better, on average, than the citizens of Baltimore. True, you can sit outside in Paris and drink little cups of coffee, but why this is more stylish than sitting inside and drinking large glasses of whiskey I don't know.

—*Holidays in Hell* (1988)

While you're in France, touch all the paintings in the Louvre to make sure they're real. The French will want to know if they aren't.

—*Modern Manners* (1983)

GERMANY

You can always reason with a German. You can always reason with a barnyard animal, too, for all the good it does.

—*Holidays in Hell* (1988)

GLOBAL POLITICS

An excess of international leadership usually results in bullets and breadlines.

—*The CEO of the Sofa* (2001)

Maybe the world has become rich enough to be bored by global politics. This is good. Politics cause more grief than money.

—*The CEO of the Sofa* (2001)

Certain nations seem to exist strictly to torment their neighbors or their citizens or both. Other nations are simply . . .

there. People go to cafés and just sit around all day. It gives an American the heebie-jeebies. We have to be making and doing. Albeit what we make is often a mess. And what we do is often our undoing.

—*Don't Vote—It Just Encourages the Bastards* (2010)

"Better red than dead!" they shrieked. They could have gone to Stalin's Russia, Mao's China, or Pol Pot's Cambodia and been both.

—*The CEO of the Sofa* (2001)

HEADS OF STATE

A desire to adore a head of state is a grim transgression against republicanism. It is worse than having a head of state who demands to be adored. It is worse even than the forced adoration of the state itself.

—*Give War a Chance* (1992)

HONG KONG

Hong Kong is a styling city, up on the trends. Truly up, in the case of platform sneakers. You can spend an entertaining afternoon on Hollywood Road watching teens fall off their shoes.

—*Eat the Rich* (1998)

Hong Kong has no forests, mines, or oil wells, no large-scale agriculture, and definitely no places to park. Hong Kong even has to import water. So in Hong Kong they drink cognac instead, more per person than anywhere else in the world. They own more Rolls-Royces per person, too. So what if there's no space at the curb? They'll hire somebody fresh from the mainland to drive around the block all night.

—*Eat the Rich* (1998)

ICELAND

Icelanders respect nature so much they've given their beavers MFAs.

—*Holidays in Heck* (2011)

INDIA

Tourism is a pointless activity. Pointless activity is a highly developed craft in India.

—*The CEO of the Sofa* (2001)

You never have to wonder where the toilet is in India, you're standing on it.

—*The CEO of the Sofa* (2001)

IRAQ

If we want to demoralize the population of Iraq and sap their will to fight, we ought to show them videotapes of the South

Bronx, Detroit City and the West Side of Chicago. Take a look, you Iraqis—this is what we do to our own cities in peacetime. Just think what we're going to do to yours in a war.

—*Give War a Chance* (1992)

We keep hearing about Iraq's "elite Republican Guard." Well, if they're so elite why don't they have better jobs than sitting around getting the stuffing bombed out of them in Kuwait? And what are they guarding anyway—big charred wrecks of buildings and blown-up bridges? And one more thing—how many of these elite Republican guards are really still Republicans?

—*Give War a Chance* (1992)

IRELAND

Agreement is something the Irish can always overcome.

—*Give War a Chance* (1992)

ISRAEL

Israel is hated fanatically by millions of Muslims around the world, whereas the U.S. Congress is loathed by only a small number of well-informed people who follow politics closely. But a walk around anything in Israel is less impeded by barriers and armed guards than a walk around the Capitol Building in Washington.

—*Peace Kills* (2004)

ITALY

The Italians have had two thousand years to fix up the Forum and just look at the place.

—*Holidays in Hell* (1988)

My daughter turned two in Venice. There, in the middle of Saint Mark's Square, a Japanese tourist lady handed her an open bag of pigeon feed and every feathered rat in Europe descended on the poor tyke.

—*Holidays in Heck* (2011)

For a city named after a brown bag lunch, Bologna has some remarkable restaurants.

—*Age and Guile Beat Youth, Innocence, and
a Bad Haircut* (1995)

KABUL

At the sunny end of the political spectrum was the National Islamic Front of Afghanistan, NIFA, headed by Syed Ahmed Gailani . . . He and his supporters are prosperous, sophisticated, well dressed and articulate and enjoy discussing such things as the Rights of Man and political pluralism. It will come as no surprise to students of journalism that the foreign reporters had made NIFA a laughingstock and called it the Gucci Front. Journalists worship authenticity the way governments worship expediency. The Gailani bunch obviously wasn't dirty and incomprehensible enough to be real Afghan freedom fighters.

—Parliament of Whores (1991)

KUWAIT

The Iraqi army is systematically blowing up buildings in downtown Kuwait City. If the architecture in Kuwait resembles the architecture in Saudi Arabia, the Iraqi army will have done one good deed, anyway. As soon as the Iraqis have all surrendered, let's send them to New York and let them take a whack at Trump Tower.

—Give War a Chance (1992)

The traffic coming toward me was made up of refugees. I guess I'd expected them to be pushing all their belongings in baby carriages the way movie newsreel refugees always were when I was a kid. These were affluent refugees—at least they had been until recently—in Chevrolet Caprice Classics, 200-series Mercedes, Peugeots and BMWs. And they were very modern refugees, people making a run for it not because Stukas were strafing their villages but because their bank cards wouldn't work in Kuwaiti cash machines anymore.

—Give War a Chance (1992)

KYRGYZSTAN

I wasn't in the Westernized, cosmopolitan part of Kyrgyzstan— such as it is—with hospitals and ambulances. I was in the part with no roads, electricity, or cell towers. A satellite phone was in my saddlebag, but I couldn't get a satellite connection. Even by the standards of outer space Kyrgyzstan is remote.

—*Holidays in Heck* (2011)

I was standing in the stirrups, stretched over the horse's neck. The reins were clenched in my teeth. I was gripping the mane with my left hand and swinging a quirt with my right, whipping the horse up a steep, grassy mountainside. There were hundreds of feet to climb to the top and a thousand feet to fall to the bottom. It had been raining all night. The grass was slick. Hooves churned. Forelegs milled in the air. Hind legs buckled. The horse was on the verge of flipping backward. And that was the least of my worries. In the first place, I don't know how to ride.

—*Holidays in Heck* (2011)

If something happened to my horse it would be shot. For me, the medical treatment wouldn't be that sophisticated.

—*Holidays in Heck* (2011)

LATIN AMERICA

The usual choice in Latin America is oppression combined with economically disastrous corruption causing a left-wing insurgency versus incompetence combined with economically disastrous social programs causing a right-wing coup.

—*Give War a Chance* (1992)

In Latin America—as in any good soap opera—the worse a situation is, the longer it lasts.

—*Give War a Chance* (1992)

LEBANON

Beirut, at a glance, lacks charm. The garbage has not been picked up since 1975. The ocean is thick with raw sewage, and trash dots the surf. Leeches have been known to pop out the tap. Electricity is intermittent. It is a noisy town. Most shops have portable gasoline generators set out on the sidewalk. The racket from these combines with incessant horn-honking, scattered gunfire, loud Arab music from pushcart cassette vendors, much yelling among the natives and occasional car bombs. Israeli jets also come in from the sea most afternoons, breaking the sound barrier on their way to targets in the Bekáa Valley. A dense brown haze from dump fires and car exhaust covers the city. Air pollution probably approaches a million parts per million. This, however, dulls the sense of smell.

—*Holidays in Hell* (1988)

Beirut nightlife is not elaborate, but it is amusing. When danger waits the tables and death is the busboy, it adds zest to the simple pleasures of life. There's poignant satisfaction in every puff of a cigarette or sip of a martini. The jokes are funnier, the drinks are stronger, the bonds of affection more powerfully felt than they'll ever be at Club Med.

—*Holidays in Hell* (1988)

"Kill them all—Let God sort them out" T-shirts are popular with the militias.

—*Holidays in Hell* (1988)

LENIN'S TOMB

It's real dark and chilly in there, and you march around three sides of the glass case, and it's like a visit to the nocturnal-predators section at the Reptile House with your grade-school class—no talking!

—*Republican Party Reptile* (1987)

MANKIND'S PROGRESS

Mankind has made improvements in living conditions over the past couple of million years. (Some people don't think so. To those people I say: dentistry.)

—*Don't Vote—It Just Encourages the Bastards* (2010)

KARL MARX

Karl was a bit of a Baby Boomer before the fact—middle-class attorney's son, sometimes student radical, unpublished novelist and poet, "underground" journalist, sponger on a crackpot rich buddy, and talking through his hat. Karl Marx was a very smart man. *Das Kapital* is a very bad hat.

—*The Baby Boom* (2014)

Despite Karl Marx's deathbed confession that he was "just kidding," some thinkers have attempted to find a rationale, or at least a poor excuse, for existence in the social intercourse of mankind. Suffice it to say, very little comment is needed on that endeavor.

—*Age and Guile Beat Youth, Innocence, and a Bad Haircut* (1995)

MARXISM

Marxism has tremendous appeal in the Third World for exactly the same reason it had tremendous appeal to me in college. It gives you something to believe in when what surrounds you seems unbelievable. It gives you someone to blame besides yourself. It's theoretically tidy. And, best of all, it's fully imaginary so it can never be disproved.

—*Give War a Chance* (1992)

MEXICO

Mexicans have different souls than we do. There's a special heaven where Mexicans go—more brightly decorated, more highly spiced, and much cheaper than ours.

—*Age and Guile Beat Youth, Innocence, and a Bad Haircut* (1995)

Their country has been run by party hacks for sixty-five years and that party is synonymous with the government and the government is synonymous with the economy and all life is a patronage plum. If you want to know why it takes so much red tape to accomplish anything in Mexico and why, after all that red tape, the thing isn't accomplished and why nobody is surprised when it isn't, think of a 763,000-square-mile, 78-million-employee New York City Department of Motor Vehicles.

—*Age and Guile Beat Youth, Innocence, and
a Bad Haircut* (1995)

MOSCOW

Nothing shone in Moscow. Storefronts weren't lit, and there were very few storefronts. No headlights were visible. More to the point, no cars were. The city had street lamps, but as far apart as Patti Smith albums.

—*Eat the Rich* (1998)

The men wear three-piece suits with stripes the width and color used to indicate no passing on two-lane highways. Shoulder pads are as high and far apart as tractor fenders, and lapel points stick out even farther, waving in the air like baseball pennants. The neckties are as wide as the wives. These wives have, I think, covered their bodies in Elmer's and run through the boutiques of Palm Springs, buying whatever stuck. Their dresses certainly appear to be glued on—flesh-tight, no matter how vast the expanse of flesh involved. Hair is in the cumulonimbus style. Personal ornaments are astonishing in both frequency and amplitude. There was a David Bowie concert in Moscow in June 1996, and according to the *Moscow Times*, the loudest sound from the expensive seats was the rattle of jewelry.

—*Eat the Rich* (1998)

NICARAGUA

Nicaragua looks—and smells—like that paradigm of socialism, a public restroom.

—*Give War a Chance* (1992)

I hadn't come to Nicaragua prepared for such joy. Like most readers of papers and watchers of newscasts, I thought the Sandinistas were supposed to win this one. I blush to admit I accepted the results of an opinion poll taken in a country where it was illegal to hold certain opinions. You can imagine the poll-taking process: "Hello, Mr. Peasant, I'm an inquisitive and frightening stranger. God knows who I work for. Would you care to ostensibly support the dictatorship which controls every facet of your existence, or shall we put you down as in favor of the UNO opposition and just tear up your ration card right here and now?"

—*Give War a Chance* (1992)

PAKISTAN

The last Soviet troops were to be withdrawn from Afghanistan. I went to Peshawar in Pakistan's North-West Frontier Province to see what would happen. Peshawar was the principal Afghan

War "listening post," which is journalese for "place that's close, but not too close, to the action and has bottled water." Not that there wasn't action in Pakistan. There was plenty of shooting and killing. It was literary criticism. The locals were busy debating the merits of Salman Rushdie's novel *The Satanic Verses*. And their arguments were more spirited than those in the *New York Review of Books*. On February 12, 7 people were killed and 127 injured in a riot in front of the American Cultural Center in Islamabad. (Rushdie is a native of India with British citizenship whose book was published by an English corporation, so naturally the demonstrations were directed at the U.S.). . . . Sneer at the mysteries of the East if you will. Not I. I was covering a war that we won without being in it from a war zone where the principal danger to life and limb was from the use of magic realism in modern fiction.

—*Parliament of Whores* (1991)

PARAGUAY

Asunción, Paraguay, is farther from New York than Moscow. Not that it matters how far away a thing is if you don't know where it's at.

—*Give War a Chance* (1992)

Paraguay's climate is almost identical to Florida's but more comfortable since nobody has to wear a giant mouse costume to make a living.

—*Give War a Chance* (1992)

THE PHILIPPINES

The reception hall of Malacanang Palace had obviously been decorated by a Las Vegas interior designer forced to lower his standards of taste at gunpoint.

—*Republican Party Reptile* (1987)

President Marcos was holding a press conference. It was completely uninteresting to see him in person. His puffy face was opaque. There was something of Nixon to his look, but not quite as nervous, and something of Mao, but not quite as dead.

—*Republican Party Reptile* (1987)

Imelda wouldn't let anyone into the presidential palace in rubber-soled shoes. She is reputedly as crazy as a rat in a coffee can, and the statuary on the palace grounds bore that out. It looked like she had broken into a Mexican birdbath factory.

—*Republican Party Reptile* (1987)

ROGUE STATES

In the long haul of history it turns out that all states are rogue states sooner or later. We certainly were, from the point of view of the Cherokee.

—*The CEO of the Sofa* (2001)

RUSSIA

A fine place as long as you could drink like a Russian and leave like an American.

—*Republican Party Reptile* (1987)

Public transport in Russia is not for the faint of nose.

—*Eat the Rich* (1998)

Russians are a people of largeness—large bodies, large gestures, large voices. In fact, Russians are enormous. Being an average-size American in St. Petersburg is like being a girl gymnast at a Teamsters convention.

—*Eat the Rich* (1998)

Half the people were drunk—a thrashing, helpless, hello-coma kind of inebriation I saw almost nowhere on this trip except occasionally in the mirror.

—*Eat the Rich* (1998)

If you stand in line long enough the state provides goods and services. The services are out of service and the goods are no good, but food, clothing, shelter and medical care are—just barely—available.

—*Give War a Chance* (1992)

SAUDI ARABIA

Until 1918 the Arabian peninsula was ruled by the Ottoman Empire, so called because it had the same amount of intelligence and energy as a footstool.

—*Give War a Chance* (1992)

Most folks back home still don't know what Saudi Arabia looks like. Sand and camels, they think. Sand and Marlboros and Pepsi would be more like it.

—*Give War a Chance* (1992)

Eastern Saudi Arabia looks like Arizona would if Arizona had beautiful beaches. There's the same big sky, the same sparse vegetation and the same modern architecture—most of it ugly, just like in Phoenix.

—*Give War a Chance* (1992)

The religious practices and attitudes of Saudi Arabia are no more peculiar than those of Billy Graham. A church-going, small-town American from forty years ago would be perfectly familiar with the public morality here. Only the absolute segregation of the sexes would seem strange. And I'm not so sure about that.

—*Give War a Chance* (1992)

Under Shari'ah religious law, murder is considered a mere civil matter, involving monetary compensation of some kind, but theft can be punished by amputation of a hand. There's also no begging or importuning or wheedling of any kind. I don't know what they amputate for this offense, but whatever it is, I suggest we start cutting it off in New York City.

—*Give War a Chance* (1992)

The Saudi Arabian beach resort of Khafji has been retaken. Which leaves us with the question: What do Saudi Arabians do at a beach resort? The women are dressed in tents, you can't get a beer to save your life and it's hard to play beach volleyball in robes that drag on the ground. As much as I can figure, the only amusement that's ever been available in Khafji is the one we've just witnessed—shooting Iraqis.

—*Give War a Chance* (1992)

SEEING THE WORLD

See the Beautiful Grand Canyon. Okay, I see it. Okay, it's beautiful. Now what? And I have no use for vacation paradises. Take the little true love along to kick back and work on the relationship. She gets her tits sunburned. I wreck the rental car. We've got our teeth in each other's throats before you can say "lost luggage." Nor do attractions attract me. If I had a chance to visit another planet, I wouldn't want to go to Six Flags Over Mars or ride through the artificial ammonia lake in a silicone-bottomed boat at Venusian Cypress Gardens. I'd want to see the planet's principal features—what makes it tick. Well, the planet I've got a chance to visit is Earth, and Earth's principal features are chaos and war. I think I'd be a fool to spend years here and never have a look.

—*Holidays in Hell* (1988)

THE SERENGETI

Vultures on the landing strip—never a good sign.
—*Eat the Rich* (1998)

The plane flew over Mount Kilimanjaro. Hemingway begins "The Snows of Ditto" by noting that there's a frozen leopard carcass at the top. "No one has explained what the leopard was seeking at that altitude," writes Hemingway. A clean bathroom is my guess.
—*Eat the Rich* (1998)

There is an all-day, all-night rush hour of animals: Cape buffalo jam, zebra lock, and wildebeest backup. Thomson's gazelles bound about with a suspicious black swipe on their sides— enough like the Nike trademark to raise questions about sponsorship. Warthogs scuttle with their tails up straight in the air, endlessly acknowledging some foul in the game of hogball. Hyenas are all over the place, nonchalant but shifty, in little groups meandering not quite aimlessly—greasers at the mall. Hippos lie in the water holes in piles, snoring, stinking, sleeping all day. The correct translation for the Greek word "hippopotamus" is not "river horse" but "river first husband." And lions doze where they like, waking up every day or two to do that famous ecological favor of culling the weak, old, and sick. (Do lions ever debate the merits of weak versus old versus sick? "Call me oversophisticated, but I think the sick wildebeest have a certain piquancy, like a ripe cheese.")
—*Eat the Rich* (1998)

Everything I saw was also being ogled by dozens of other folks from out of town, but the tourists pay money, and money is what it takes to keep the parks and preserves more or less unspoiled, and to buy the bullets to shoot poachers. If the animals of Africa aren't worth more alive to rubberneckers than they're worth dead to farmers, pastoralists, and rhino-horn erection peddlers, then that's that for the Call of the Wild.

—*Eat the Rich* (1998)

A significant minority of creatures on the African veldt aren't grazers or browsers, or members of PETA. They're hungry, too. And buff. Running down a 500-pound herbivore is an excellent exercise program.

—*Eat the Rich* (1998)

Cheetahs and leopards will kill—as will many a lesser hunter in a duck blind—for fun. So wildebeest wake up a lot in the night, and when they wake up, they eat. They mate, of course. Once a year. Fun-o. They migrate to find other things to eat. They go to water holes, but these are haunted by crocodiles, lions, jackals, wild dogs, hyenas, and minibuses full of tourists waiting to see the violence and strong-language portions of safari. That's about it for the wildebeest lifestyle. The young ones frisk, but they get over it.

—*Eat the Rich* (1998)

There used to be thousands of rhinoceros in Tanzania. Now there are not. The poachers got the rhinos, as they've gotten most of the rhinos in Africa, all because middle-aged men in Asia believe the powdered horn gives rise—as it were—to potency. Like the world needs middle-aged men with extra hard-ons.

—*Eat the Rich* (1998)

SHANGHAI

I went to what looked like the worst pet store ever. Inside was a wall of terrariums full of fat, angry poisonous snakes, hissing, pulling hood boners, and making wet bongo noises when they tried to strike through the glass. This was, in fact, a restaurant.

—*Eat the Rich* (1998)

Omnipresent amid all the frenzy of Shanghai is that famous portrait, that modern icon. The faintly smiling, bland, yet somehow threatening visage appears in brilliant red hues on placards and posters, and is painted huge on the sides of buildings. Some call him a genius. Others blame him for the deaths of millions. There are those who say his military reputation was inflated, yet he conquered the mainland in short order. Yes, it's Colonel Sanders.

—*Eat the Rich* (1998)

SOMALIA

Somalia is amazingly roofless. Almost every building we flew over had its ceiling off. How much of this was from neglect and artillery and how much from looting of corrugated tin sheets I don't know, but you could look right down into the rooms and hallways, and it made the entire country seem like a gigantic game board of Clue. Probable correct answer: Everybody. In the toilet. With an AK-47.

—*All the Trouble in the World* (1994)

Everything that guns can accomplish had been achieved in Mogadishu.

—*All the Trouble in the World* (1994)

Before the marines came, the children were dying like . . . "Dying like flies" is not a simile you'd use in Somalia. The flies wax prosperous and lead full lives. Before the marines came, the children were dying like children.

—*All the Trouble in the World* (1994)

SOUTH AFRICA

South Africa looks like California—the same tan-to-cancer beaches—the same Granola'd mountains' majesty, the same subdeveloped bushveldt. Johannesburg looks like L.A. Like L.A., it was all built since 1900. Like L.A., it's ringed and vectored with expressways. And its best suburb, Hyde Park, looks just like Beverly Hills. All the people who live in Hyde Park are white, just like Beverly Hills. And all the people who work there—who cook, sweep and clean the swimming pools— are not white, just like Beverly Hills. The only difference is, the lady who does the laundry carries it on her head.

—*Holidays in Hell* (1988)

SPAIN

When [the Spanish] conquered the New World, they obtained tons of gold, melted it down, and sent it to the mint. It never occurred to them that they were just creating more money, not more things to spend it on. Between 1500 and 1600, prices in Spain went up 400 percent. Instead of the vast wealth of America's oceans, fields, and forests, Spain took the gold. It was as if someone robbed a bank and stole nothing but deposit slips.

—*None of My Business* (2018)

SWEDEN

I stared at the quaint, narrow houses, the clean and boring shops, the well-behaved white people. They appeared to be Disney creations—and not from the new, hip, PG-13 Disney rumored to be opening a Scotch-and-Water Park. This was the Disney of the original Disneyland. Gamla Stan had the same labored cuteness, preternatural tidiness, and inexhaustible supply of courtesy from its denizens. I half-expected to turn around and see someone dressed as Donald Duck. Instead, I turned around and saw someone dressed as the king of Sweden. Which, in fact, he was. King Carl XVI Gustaf was riding, in a gilded coach-and-four with a footman in knee breeches holding on behind, right down the middle of the street in a country renowned the world over for its utter egalitarianism.

—*Eat the Rich* (1998)

Sweden isn't like Minnesota or Disneyland, but then again, it isn't much like Sweden, either. The people aren't all that tall and blond, they don't talk orgy-borgy talk.

—*Eat the Rich* (1998)

I gathered heaps of Swedish self-seriousness. One tome was
called *Love! You Can Really Feel It, You Know!* a title I can only
hope lost something in translation. The chapter headed "The
Adolescent Years—Questions to the World" contains these
"Questions from Boys": "How big is the average dick?" and
"How many holes does a girl have?" And under "Questions
from Girls": "When will my breasts start growing?"

"When will my breasts *stop* growing?"

Not that the Swedes possess no sense of humor.

—*Eat the Rich* (1998)

The Swedish idea of spicy falls somewhere between Commu-
nion wafers and ketchup. Cream sauce is everywhere.

—*Eat the Rich* (1998)

TANZANIA

Probably every child whose parents weren't rich enough has
been told, "We're rich in other ways." Tanzania is fabulously
rich in other ways.

—*Eat the Rich* (1998)

Not that the Tanzanians didn't understand our big ideas; they
understood them too well. They just had no experience with
how bad most big ideas are. They hadn't been through Freud-
ianism, Keynesianism, liberalism, www.heavensgate.com, and
"Back to Africa." They don't have 10,000 unemployable liberal-
arts majors sitting around Starbucks with nose rings.

—*Eat the Rich* (1998)

No matter what our motives are for being appalled by Tanzanian poverty, we'd better do something about it. There's suffering humanity to be considered. And that suffering humanity will be us if we're not careful.

—*Eat the Rich* (1998)

THIRD WORLD DRIVING

It's important to understand that in the Third World most driving is done with the horn, or "Egyptian Brake Pedal," as it is known. There is a precise and complicated etiquette of horn use. Honk your horn only under the following circumstances:

1. When anything blocks the road.
2. When anything doesn't.
3. When anything might.
4. At red lights.
5. At green lights.
6. At all other times.

—*Holidays in Hell* (1988)

TOURISTS IN THE SOVIET UNION

They were leftists all right. These were people who believed everything about the Soviet Union was perfect, but they were bringing their own toilet paper.

—*Republican Party Reptile* (1987)

THE UNITED NATIONS

The only thing the United Nations is suited for is an invasion from Mars.

—The CEO of the Sofa (2001)

At the UN they put butter on their bagels. No wonder these people can't achieve peace in the Middle East.

—The CEO of the Sofa (2001)

VENICE BIENNALE

How bad does modern art stink? Every two years since 1895 (war and such allowing), the Venice Biennale has gathered new masterpieces from around the world in a place and at a season where the reek of genius can be accurately compared to the warm-weather aroma of the Grand Canal.

—Holidays in Heck (2011)

VIETNAM

Saigon was still mostly a two-wheeled city, but motorized and not just with little Honda engines. Young idiots hardballed down the avenues on 500cc café racers. Even bicycles were ridden with attitude. Traffic was like a bad dog. It wasn't important to look both ways when crossing the street; it was important to not show fear.

—All the Trouble in the World (1994)

VLADIVOSTOK

Vladivostok looks like, in the words of Russian writer Gleb Uspensky, "what could have happened to San Francisco if the Bolsheviks ever got there." Fortunately, they were stopped in Berkeley.

—*Eat the Rich* (1998)

Vladivostok should be among the Pacific Rim's foremost market-places for food, fuel, and raw materials, but Soviet military paranoia kept the docks closed to foreign trade until 1990. Now the town is notable only for Chinese border smuggling, Mafia activity, trash on the beach (Vladidumpstok), and a Japanese restaurant with the second-worst-imaginable name: "Nagasaki."

—*Eat the Rich* (1998)

WAR

War is steroids and free weights for government.
—*The CEO of the Sofa* (2001)

WAR AND PEACE

Peacenik types say there would be no war if people truly understood how horrible war is. They're wrong. People don't mind a little horror. They can even be enthusiastic about it if the horror is happening to somebody else.

—*Give War a Chance* (1992)

If people truly understood how much sleeping on rocks, how much eating things rejected by high school cafeterias, how much washing small parts of the body in cold water and how much sheer sitting around in the dirt war entails, we might have world peace after all.

—*Give War a Chance* (1992)

At dawn on Thursday, March 20, when the first American missiles struck Baghdad, I was asleep in a big, soft bed. My wife, watching late-night news in the United States, called me in Kuwait to tell me the war had started. That was embarrassing for a professional journalist in a combat zone. But I looked around my comfortable hotel room and thought, "We *are* fighting for freedom. In this case, the freedom to go back to sleep in a big, soft bed."

—*Peace Kills* (2004)

War will exist as long as there's a food chain.

—*Holidays in Hell* (1988)

WORLD CONSPIRACIES

There are no conspiracies that rule the world. There's no universe-mastering cabal of capitalists, communists, Islamic fundamentalists, International Monetary Fund executives, Federal Reserve Bank governors, New World Order functionaries with their UN black helicopters, Trilateral Commission initiates, Freemasons, Bavarian Illuminati, Rosicrucians, Knights Templar, Mafia families, Chinese triads, Mexican drug

gangs, Jesuits, or Google. And no, no, no, no, it's not the Jews.
They'd do a better job.

—*Don't Vote—It Just Encourages the Bastards* (2010)

XENOPHOBIA

Back in London, I was having dinner in the Groucho Club—
this week's in-spot for what's left of Britain's lit glitz and
nouveau rock *riche*—when one more person started in on the
Stars and Stripes. Eventually he got, as the Europeans always
do, to the part about "Your country's never been invaded."
(This fellow had been two during the Blitz, you see.) "You
don't know the horror, the suffering. You think war is . . ."

I snapped.

"A John Wayne movie," I said. "That's what you were going
to say, wasn't it? We think war is a John Wayne movie. We think
life is a John Wayne movie—with good guys and bad guys, as
simple as that. Well, you know something, Mister Limey Poof-
ter? You're right. And let me tell you who those bad guys are.
They're *us*. WE BE BAD.

"We're the baddest-assed sons of bitches that ever jogged
in Reeboks. We're three-quarters grizzly bear and two-thirds
car wreck and descended from a stock market crash on our
mother's side. You take your Germany, France and Spain, roll
them all together and it wouldn't give us room to park our
cars. We're the big boys, Jack, the original, giant, economy-
sized, new and improved butt kickers of all time. When
we snort coke in Houston, people lose their hats in Cap
d'Antibes. And we've got an American Express card credit
limit higher than your piss-ant metric numbers go.

"You say our country's never been invaded? You're right,
little buddy. Because I'd like to see the needle-dicked foreigners

who'd have the guts to try. We drink napalm to get our hearts started in the morning. A rape and a mugging is our way of saying 'Cheerio.' Hell can't hold our sock-hops. We walk taller, talk louder, spit further, fuck longer and buy more things than you know the names of. I'd rather be a junkie in a New York City jail than king, queen and jack of all you Europeans. We eat little countries like this for breakfast and shit them out before lunch."

Of course, the guy should have punched me. But this was Europe. He just smiled his shabby, superior European smile.

(God, don't these people have *dentists?*)

—*Holidays in Hell* (1988)

PART IV

REAL LIFE

I believe that Western civilization, after some disgusting glitches, has become almost civilized. I believe it is our first duty to protect that civilization. I believe it is our second duty to improve it. I believe it is our third duty to extend it if we can. But let's be careful about that last point. Not everybody is ready to be civilized. I wasn't in 1969.

—Give War a Chance (1992)

We are left trying to weigh the delicate balance between having a life worth living and having a planet that can support life.

—A Cry from the Far Middle (2020)

AGRICULTURE

Like that of most Americans of the present generation, my experience with agriculture is pretty much limited to one three-week experiment raising dead marijuana plants under a grow light in the closet of my off-campus apartment. I did, however, once help artificially inseminate a cow. And you can keep your comments to yourself—I was up at the front, holding the thing's head.

Getting a cow in a family way is not accomplished, as I would have thought, with a bull and some Barry White tapes in a heart-shaped stall. It's like teenage pregnancy, only more so. The bull isn't even around to get the cow knocked-up. Instead, there's a liquid-nitrogen Thermos bottle full of frozen bull sperm (let's not even think about how they get that) and a device resembling a cross between a gigantic hypodermic needle and the douche nozzle of the gods.

My old friend George got a real farmer to come by and actually do the honors. So while I held the cow's head and George held the cow's middle, the real farmer, Pete, took the bovine marital aid and inserted it into a very personal and private place of the cow's. Then Pete squirted liquid dish soap on himself and inserted his right arm into an even more personal and private place of the cow's, all the way up to the elbow. Pete did this not in order to have Robert Mapplethorpe take his photograph, but in order to grasp the inseminator tube through the intestine wall and guide the tube into the mouth of the uterus. It's an alarming thing to watch, and I'm glad to say I didn't watch it because I was at the cow's other end. But I'll tell you this, I will never forget the look on that cow's face.

—*Parliament of Whores* (1991)

CHARITY

The problem with charity is that people can be remarkably hard to help.

—None of My Business (2018)

CHILDREN

I teach them about hypocrisy. I teach by example.

—A Cry from the Far Middle (2020)

Children—lucky children at least—live in that ideal state postulated by Marx, where the rule is, "From each according to his abilities, to each according to his needs." Getting grounded equals being sent to a gulag. Dad in high dudgeon is confused with Joseph Stalin. Then we wonder why so many young people are leftists.

—Eat the Rich (1998)

Nothing is more embarrassing to children than "hip" parents. Remember the poor fellow in high school whose mother wore miniskirts and whose father claimed to "dig" the Beatles?

—The CEO of the Sofa (2001)

My middle child already knows as much as she cares to know about whatever you want to teach her. "Whatever," in fact, is her particular favorite word. "I know the alphabet—A, B, G, D, whatever."

—Holidays in Heck (2011)

There are some things upon which it is difficult to place a value. This is why we don't use money to measure all of our exchanges. Kids get food, clothing, and shelter from parents, and in return, parents get . . . kids.

—*Eat the Rich* (1998)

The real truth about children is they don't speak the language very well. They're physically uncoordinated. And they are ignorant of our elaborate ideas about right and wrong.

—*The Bachelor Home Companion* (1987)

Children are actually very interesting. They'd probably be worth reporting on if they got their own country or something.

—*Holidays in Heck* (2011)

I caught my six-year-old playing "health care provider" with one of the little girls in his first-grade class. They were filling out toy forms fully clothed.

—*Don't Vote—It Just Encourages the Bastards* (2010)

The kindly bachelor thinks, "We'd be more understanding with an adult who was a foreigner or hopelessly clumsy or from another planet." But would we really be more understanding with an all-thumbs extra-terrestrial who spoke nothing but French and didn't know the golden retriever puppy wasn't supposed to go in the washing machine? And what if he came to live with us for eighteen years?

—*The Bachelor Home Companion* (1987)

Social media makes our kids into victims of bullies or perpetrators of bullying—depending on whether our kids are dorks or jerks, and in my experience every kid is both.

—*A Cry from the Far Middle* (2020)

To my children Facebook is about as interesting and hip as the school bulletin board. They have ways of electronically communicating with their peers that are so new, so devious, so incomprehensible to adults that, by comparison, the German Enigma machine was a secret decoder ring in a Cracker Jack box.

—*None of My Business* (2018)

CIVILIZATION

We must give civilization its due. The Latin root of the word "civilization" is civitas, "city." You can't have civilization without cities. Watch reruns of *Hee Haw* for proof.

—*None of My Business* (2018)

CLEANLINESS

Cleanliness becomes more important at moments when godliness is not possible.

—*Modern Manners* (1983)

CLIMATE CHANGE

There are 1.3 billion people in China, and they all want a Buick. Actually, if you go more than a mile or two outside China's big cities, the wants are more basic. People want a hot plate and a piece of methane-emitting cow to cook on it. They want a carbon-belching moped, and some CO_2-disgorging heat in their houses in the winter. And air-conditioning wouldn't be considered an imposition, if you've ever been to China in the summer. Now, I want you to dress yourself in sturdy clothing and go tell 1.3 billion Chinese they can never have a Buick. Then, assuming the Sierra Club helicopter has rescued you in time, I want you to go tell a billion people in India the same thing.

—*Don't Vote—It Just Encourages the Bastards* (2010)

CONFORMITY

Whenever I'm in the middle of conformity, surrounded by oneness of mind with people oozing concurrence on every side, I get scared. And when I find myself agreeing with everybody, too, I get terrified.

—*Parliament of Whores* (1991)

DANGER

There are certain subjects about which people are incurable boneheads. Humans apparently cannot rationally consider what constitutes a danger to humanity or how likely any given danger is to occur.

—*Parliament of Whores* (1991)

DEATH

It's hard to face the truth but I suppose you yourself realize that if you'd had just a little more courage, just a little more strength of character, you could have been dead by now. No such luck.

—Republican Party Reptile (1987)

Death is a handy reminder of how many environmental problems aren't simply problems, they're costs. Population pressure, for example, is the cost we pay for not being dead.

—The CEO of the Sofa (2001)

Transformations in healthcare have turned the historically cheapest part of being alive—dying—into something so expensive that many people can't afford to do it.

—A Cry from the Far Middle (2020)

ECOLOGY

Ecological problems won't be solved by special interest groups spreading pop hysteria and merchandising fashionable panic. Genuine hard-got knowledge is required. The collegiate idealists who fill the ranks of the environmental movement seem willing to do absolutely anything to save the biosphere, except take science courses and learn something about it. In 1971 American universities awarded 4,390 doctorates in the physical sciences. After fifteen years of youthful fretting over the planet's future, the number was 3,551.

—Parliament of Whores (1991)

Not all lessons in ecology are edifying. The marine iguana, for example. Washing ashore from the mainland, it learned to go with the flow. It became the only seagoing lizard. It eats nothing but algae. Here is the lizard version of moving to Humboldt County, California, growing your own vegetables, and weaving your clothes from hemp. Marine iguanas are as dull as folk songs and as ugly as unglazed pottery. They spend all day lying on top of each other in big iguana group gropes.

—*Holidays in Heck* (2011)

ECONOMICS

Microeconomics is about money you don't have, and macroeconomics is about money the government is out of.

—*Eat the Rich* (1998)

Not believing in the marketplace is akin to not believing in gravity.

—*The CEO of the Sofa* (2001)

Watching people try to kill each other teaches important economic lessons.

—*None of My Business* (2018)

I make no claim to understand economics. But I have begun to understand how economics is understood. This is how economics is understood after two semesters at most colleges:

I. There are a lot of graphs.

II. I'd better memorize them.

III. Or get last year's test.

And this is how economics is understood after three drinks at most bars:

I. There are only so many things in the world, and somebody is taking my share.

II. All payment for work is underpayment.

III. All business is crime.

    A. Retailers are thieves.

    B. Wholesalers are pimps.

    C. Manufacturers are slave drivers.

IV. All wealth is the result of criminal conspiracy among:

    A. Jews.

    B. Japanese.

    C. Pirates in neckties on Wall Street.

—*Eat the Rich* (1998)

ECONOMIC THEORY

I subjected myself to a large dose of economic theory because I'd finally realized that money was as important as love or death. I thought I would learn all about money. But money turns out to be strange, insubstantial, and practically impossible to define. Then I began to understand that economic theory was really about value. But value is something that's personal and relative, and changes all the time. Money can't be valued. And value can't be priced. I should never have worried that I didn't know what I was talking about. Economics is an entire scientific discipline of not knowing what you're talking about.

—*Eat the Rich* (1998)

EDUCATION

Maybe you shouldn't get an education after all. I'm not well educated enough to know.

—*Age and Guile Beat Youth, Innocence, and a Bad Haircut* (1995)

I was an English major or, as people in business call it, stupid.

—*Don't Vote—It Just Encourages the Bastards* (2010)

Examine any history textbook assigned in schools to see the "Memory Hole" at work on a scale undreamed of by *1984*'s protagonist Winston Smith doing his job at the Ministry of Truth turning former luminaries into "unpersons." Sally Hemings is now more revered than Thomas Jefferson.

—*None of My Business* (2018)

I have told my children that I never took drugs, never had sex until I was married to their mom, and that when I was a kid I made my bed every morning before I left for school.

If the kids believe that, they'll believe anything. They might even believe in getting a good education.

—*A Cry from the Far Middle* (2020)

THE END OF STRANGE

Almost nothing looks strange to anyone. A contemporary teen-ager's mother will return from a Plasmatics concert featuring Wendy O. Williams and ask her daughter, "What about flesh-colored latex Capri pants and nipple Band-Aids—would it look good on me?"

—*Modern Manners* (1983)

ENVIRONMENTALISTS

The beliefs of many environmentalists have little to do with the welfare of the globe or the well-being of its inhabitants and a lot to do with the parlor primitivism of the Romantic movement. There is this horrible idea, beginning with Jean-Jacques Rousseau and still going strong in college classrooms, that natural man is naturally good. All we have to do is strip away the neuroses, repressions and Dial soap of modern society, and mankind will return to an Edenic state. Anybody who's ever met a toddler knows this is nonsense. (Though Rousseau may not have—the five children he had by his mistress Thérèse Levasseur were sent to orphanages at birth.)

—*Parliament of Whores* (1991)

ETERNITY

Everyone wants to live forever, and a couple of bored kids can make one rainy Saturday afternoon seem like eternity.

—*The CEO of the Sofa* (2001)

EXISTENCE

The engine of existence is fueled by just a few things. Unglazed pottery is not among them.

—*Eat the Rich* (1998)

FAILURE

Failure is necessary to evolution but equally necessary to creationism.

—*Don't Vote—It Just Encourages the Bastards* (2010)

THE "FAIRNESS PRECEPT"

My eldest daughter is a child much given to exclamations of "That's not fair!" One day, when she was about eight or nine and had worked herself into a huge snit about the unfairness of something or other, I lost my patience and snapped at her. "Not fair?" I said. "You're cute. That's not fair. Your parents are pretty well off. That's not fair. You were *born in America.* THAT'S not fair. You'd better pray things don't start getting *fair* for you!"

—*A Cry from the Far Middle* (2020)

FAITH

CH RCH TODAY
WHAT'S MISSING?
U ARE

—*The Baby Boom* (2014)

FAMILY LOVE

Family love is messy, clinging, and of an annoying and repetitive pattern, like bad wallpaper.

—*Modern Manners* (1983)

FATHERLY ADVICE

Perhaps your own dad, when you were of a suitable age, took you into his den, loaded up his pipe, looked over the top of his reading glasses, and said, "If it flies, floats, or fucks—*rent it.*"

—*Age and Guile Beat Youth, Innocence, and a Bad Haircut* (1995)

FURNITURE

I look around my house and everything except the kids and dogs is made in China.

—*Don't Vote—It Just Encourages the Bastards* (2010)

GOD

Central to the concept of God (or Gods) in every faith is that He (or They) knows (or know) exactly what we're up to at all times and why. This should be terrifying, but most people who are religious—myself included—seem more comforted than frightened by God's omniscience.

—*None of My Business* (2018)

The word "fun" is not found anywhere in the Bible—no surprise to a Catholic.

—*Holidays in Heck* (2011)

GOD, EVOLUTION, AND THE UNIVERSE

I believe in God. I also believe in evolution. If death weren't around to "finalize" the Darwinian process, we'd all still be amoebas. We'd eat by surrounding pizzas with our belly flab and have sex by lying on railroad tracks waiting for a train to split us into significant others. I consider evolution to be more than a scientific theory. I think it's a call to God. God created a free universe. He could have created any kind of universe He wanted. But a universe without freedom would have been static and meaningless—a taxpayer-funded-art-in-public-places universe.

—*Holidays in Heck* (2011)

THE GREATEST GENERATION?

I've about had it with this "greatest generation" malarkey. You people have one stock market crash in 1929, and it takes you a dozen years to go get a job. Then you wait until Germany and Japan have conquered half the world before it occurs to you to get involved in World War II. After that you get surprised by a million Red Chinese in Korea. Where do you put a million Red Chinese so they'll be a surprise? You spend the entire 1950s watching Lawrence Welk and designing

tail fins. You come up with the idea for Vietnam. Thanks. And
you elect Richard Nixon. The hell with you.

—The CEO of the Sofa (2001)

GUILT

The confessional tendency in modern society is reputed by
psychiatrists to be the result of a guilt neurosis concerning
excess personal liberty and the breakdown of traditional values
and so on. This is not true. It's just that the only way we can
get anyone to listen to us when we talk about ourselves is by
turning that talk into gossip of the most horrid kind possible.

—Modern Manners (1983)

HONEYMOONS

When the groom farts in front of the bride, the honeymoon
is over.

—Age and Guile Beat Youth, Innocence, and a Bad Haircut (1995)

IGNORANCE

It can be hard for those of us with SAT scores exceeding our
golf handicaps to remember that ignorance is a renewable
resource.

—Give War a Chance (1992)

IMPORTANT PEOPLE

An important person should be treated exactly like anyone else holding a gun at your head.

—*Modern Manners* (1983)

INEQUITY

A soaring economy has left unconscionable deprivation in the midst of ridiculous luxury. A click on a web site can now deliver everything to everybody—except a living wage.

—*A Cry from the Far Middle* (2020)

INHERITANCE

Rich parents are famous both for miserliness and astonishing longevity. And, when they finally do die, you'll find they've left their estate in inviolate trust to the golden retrievers.

—*Modern Manners* (1983)

INNOVATION

It's all right not to get out of your chair. It gives you time to think. The most important innovations are ideas. Don't just do something, sit there.

—*None of My Business* (2018)

IRONY

Life is full of ironies for the stupid.

—*Parliament of Whores* (1991)

JARGON

Lust, Pride, Sloth, and Gluttony, or, as we call them these days, "getting in touch with your sexuality," "raising your self-esteem," "relaxation therapy," and "being a recovered bulimic."

—*The CEO of the Sofa* (2001)

JESUS

"I found Jesus," my sister announced.
  "Were you playing hide-and-seek?"

—*The Baby Boom* (2014)

Jesus is quoted as using the word "happy" only once, on the occasion of washing his disciples' feet. We admire the Son of Man but we sons of a gun who populate America do not pursue our happiness in this manner.

—*Don't Vote—It Just Encourages the Bastards* (2010)

JUSTICE

Society holds trials for the same reason that Shakespeare had comic relief in *Macbeth*. So try to make everyone laugh. Pleading innocent is usually the best way to do this.

—*Modern Manners* (1983)

JUSTIFICATION

There is something more horrible than hoodlums, churls and vipers, and this is knaves with moral justification for their cause.

—*Give War a Chance* (1992)

LIES

The phrase "to lie with a straight face" is prolix. All lies are told with a straight face. It's truth that's said with a dismissive giggle.

—*Give War a Chance* (1992)

LIQUID ADULTHOOD

Alcohol is very important for young people because it provides a sort of "liquid adulthood." If you are young and you drink a great deal it will spoil your health, slow your mind, make you fat—in other words, turn you into an adult.

—*Modern Manners* (1983)

LONGEVITY

Millions of us are leading empty, useless, pitiful lives and lifting weights and eating fiber to make those lives last longer.

> —*Age and Guile Beat Youth, Innocence, and a Bad Haircut* (1995)

LOVE

You fall in love with perhaps half a dozen people in your life, and a like number of people fall in love with you. But the affections are rarely mutual and almost never contemporary. It is the most irresponsible thing that can be done to let such a coincidence pass and not act upon it. Of course, I didn't know that. I thought that the world was infinitely supplied with romances and that I would be the willing recipient of each in its turn. I was very young. But ignorance of natural law is a weaker excuse even than ignorance of the criminal code.

> —*Age and Guile Beat Youth, Innocence, and a Bad Haircut* (1995)

Love is much discussed but little practiced.

> —*Modern Manners* (1983)

MAKING THE WORLD A BETTER PLACE

You have to be careful. When you try to make the world a better place, you're assuming that you know what the world needs, that you know what the world should be doing, that you know what everyone in the world wants. I don't even know what *I* want.

—*None of My Business* (2018)

MANNERS

Good manners are a combination of intelligence, education, taste, and style mixed together so that you don't need any of those things. Good manners have a number of distinctive qualities: First, they can be learned by rote. This is a good thing; otherwise most rich men's daughters could not be displayed in public.

—*Modern Manners* (1983)

MEMORY

For a purely untrustworthy human organ, the memory is right in there with the penis.

—*Age and Guile Beat Youth, Innocence, and a Bad Haircut* (1995)

Sure, everyone says the Sixties were fun. Down at the American Legion hall everybody says World War II was fun, if you talk to them after 10:00 P.M.

—*Age and Guile Beat Youth, Innocence, and a Bad Haircut* (1995)

I envision a dramatic national campaign. Slogan: ALZHEIMER'S—FERGEDABOUDIT!

—*The CEO of the Sofa* (2001)

MENACE TO CIVILIZATION

There is one menace to western civilization, one assault on
the free world, one threat to everything we value. I speak of the
childproof bottle top. Now a childproof bottle top is a fine
thing for a child who has no job or other weighty responsibilities in life and can spend all day mastering the technique of
opening bleach and cleaning-fluid containers. But an aspirin
bottle equipped with such a device is a Gordian knot to an
adult who drinks.

—*Republican Party Reptile* (1987)

MIDDLE-AGE PROBLEMS

Middle-age problems—kids, indigestion, baldness—stop only
in the Alzheimer's care facility or the cardiac ward. You can't
get away from things that won't *go* away.

—*The CEO of the Sofa* (2001)

The way to deal with plane crashes is by making a list: back
taxes owed, alimony due, yard chores outstanding, amount
of school tuition to be paid next year, net loss when Crampon
Inc. went into Chapter 11, date of next scheduled colonos-
copy, etc. Then, if the plane gets into trouble, I pull out this
piece of paper and die smiling.

—*The CEO of the Sofa* (2001)

MODERN

Modern—the word is now mainly used on tags at yard sales to increase the price of ugly lamps. Modern lamps were the product of Modern Design, which was the product of Modern Art, a product that turned ugly because its producers thought art should constantly change. Art quickly ran out of things to change into that weren't stupid.

—*The CEO of the Sofa* (2001)

MOVED TO TEARS

The audience that's easily moved to tears is as easily moved to sadistic dementia. People are not thinking under such circumstances.

—*Give War a Chance* (1992)

NATURE

Nature, I'm sad to report, is woefully underdeveloped in an economic sense. The wildlife herds are sad reminders that there are only two ways to obtain a thing; either agree upon a price for it or take it by butting heads. Wildebeest must depend upon the latter method. Due to a lack of pockets, wildebeest cannot carry cash or credit cards. Among animals, only marsupials have pockets, and then just to keep their young inside. And there are various difficulties, practical and theoretical, with an economic system based on inch-long blind and hairless kangaroos.

—*Eat the Rich* (1998)

Why do people spend so little time contemplating the ugliness of nature? A Jamaican fruit bat looks like a colonel in the rat air force. And it's got a set of teeth on it that you could use to perform an appendectomy. If I were Jamaican, I'd keep the fruit out in the garage or maybe rent a mini-storage space.

—*All the Trouble in the World* (1994)

NEOLITHIC MAN

Neolithic man was not a fellow who always left his camp site cleaner than he found it. Ancient humans blighted half the earth with indiscriminate use of fire for slash-and-burn agriculture and hunting drives. They caused desertification through overgrazing and woodcutting in North Africa, the Middle East and China. And they were responsible for the extinction of mammoths, mastodons, cave bears, giant sloths, New World camels and horses and thousands of other species. Their record on women's issues and minority rights wasn't great either.

—*Parliament of Whores* (1991)

THE NEW TESTAMENT

The New Testament, arguably the founding text of Western civilization, mentions happiness just seven times and never in a happy context.

—*Don't Vote—It Just Encourages the Bastards* (2010)

NONCONFORMITY

Nonconformists long ago exhausted the supply of stuff with which not to conform. They've been reduced to wearing tongue studs.

—*The CEO of the Sofa* (2001)

NOT MY FAULT

A gigantic global "Not My Fault" project has been undertaken with heroic amounts of time, effort, and money devoted to psychology, psychotherapy, sociology, sociopaths, social work, social sciences, Scientology, science, chemistry, the brain, brain chemistry, serotonin reuptake inhibitors, inhibitions, sex, sex therapy, talk therapy, talk radio, talk radio personalities, personality disorders, drugs, drug-free school zones, Internet addiction, economics, the Fed, PMS, SATs, IQ, DNA, evolution, abortion, divorce, no-fault car insurance, the Democratic Party, diagnosis of attention deficit disorder in small boys . . . The list goes on.

—*Don't Vote—It Just Encourages the Bastards* (2010)

NUNS

Did they have hair? Did they have *feet?*

—*The Baby Boom* (2014)

OTHER PEOPLE

If you find yourself with strangers or people you don't know
well and you want to break the ice, ask them if they'd like to
screw. This is flattering, concerns them personally, and will
lead to lots of interesting gossip.

—*Modern Manners* (1983)

We never listen to what people we can't stand are saying.
—*The CEO of the Sofa* (2001)

If the earth's population ever runs off a cliff, it will probably be
because we've all decided to take up hang gliding at the same
time.

—*The CEO of the Sofa* (2001)

No matter how idiotic you are there are bigger idiots out there.
—*None of My Business* (2018)

The one thing that can be safely said about the great majority
of people is that we don't want them around. Be sincere and
forthright about the problem. Take the person you want to get
rid of aside and tell him he has to leave because the people
you're with hate him. Say, "I'm sorry, Fred, but you can't sit
down with us. Molly and Bill Dinnersworth hate you because
you're so much smarter and more successful than they are."
This is nasty and flattering at the same time. And it makes life
more interesting, which, if you're too sophisticated to just want
attention, is the point of existence.

—*Modern Manners* (1983)

PERFECTION

People said they were a perfect couple. Perhaps they were. They were a little too vivid, like all perfect things, and like all perfect things they were destined for destruction. (And it is invariably satisfying to note that all perfect things are destined for destruction. Unfortunately, all imperfect things are destined for destruction also.)

—*Age and Guile Beat Youth, Innocence, and
a Bad Haircut* (1995)

Anyone who thinks that cars add to greenhouse gases and horses do not hasn't spent enough time behind a horse.

—*Don't Vote—It Just Encourages
the Bastards* (2010)

PREJUDICE

I've had to endure enormous prejudice. True, since I'm a middle-aged white male Republican, the enormous prejudice came from me.

—*The CEO of the Sofa* (2001)

PRIESTS

Priests, performing the mumbo jumbo of the Latin Mass, were almost as impressive as stage magicians.

—*The Baby Boom* (2014)

A Catholic priest could probably pull a quarter out of your ear. (That he could do something else in some other place of yours was not yet a popular article of faith.)

—*The Baby Boom* (2014)

THE RICH

We allow a great deal of latitude to the rich. This is our way of making it up to them for creating a society in which everything can be had for money, but nothing is worth having.

—*Modern Manners* (1983)

Are Rich Families Better? Not necessarily and especially not in America. The dignity evaporates when you discover they made their fortune in dog laxatives.

—*Modern Manners* (1983)

SALVATION

The great religions regard us as individuals, treating sin and salvation as individual matters, at least most of the time. There are occasional group discounts, such as with the Sixth Commandment. Thou shalt not kill—unless you all get together and attack the Canaanites. We Christians don't say our prayers as if we were responding to random polling of the likely blessed with a plus or minus five percent margin of error on "Thy will be done." Buddhists don't have a graduated meditation rate that shifts the burden of enlightenment to those with greater assets in the sitter department. And Allah doesn't welcome believers into paradise saying, "You weren't a good Muslim, but you were standing in a crowd of good Muslims when you detonated the explosives in your suicide vest."

—*Don't Vote—It Just Encourages the Bastards* (2010)

SECRETS

People are so liable to tell secrets that if they don't have any embarrassing secrets to tell about themselves, they'll make up some.

—*Don't Vote—It Just Encourages the Bastards* (2010)

SELF-LOATHING/LOVE

Self-loathing is one of those odd, illogical leaps of human intuition that is almost always correct.

—*Give War a Chance* (1992)

Of course self-love cannot be displayed in full bloom without a leafy green background of hatred for others.

—*Give War a Chance* (1992)

SOCIAL CHANGE

We're undergoing social changes so swift and profound that they send even the best cultural anthropologists fleeing. A latter-day Margaret Mead would be hiding out in Samoa, hoping like heck to study something as relatively uncomplicated as teenagers.

—*A Cry from the Far Middle* (2020)

STEPFATHERS

My stepfather decided to teach me a lesson, too. He sold my Ford, emptied my save-up-for-an-MGA bank account, and declared I'd never drive another of the household vehicles as long as he lived. Which wasn't long. He got cancer in 1965, and I remember the words I used to comfort my mother the night he passed away. "Mom," I said, "can I borrow the car?"

—*The CEO of the Sofa* (2001)

STYLE

A hat should be taken off when you greet a lady and left off for the rest of your life. Nothing looks more stupid than a hat.

—*Modern Manners* (1983)

Belts should not have buckles the size of hubcaps or your name across the back. Personalizations, such as monograms and so on, should also be eschewed. If you're anyone important, people already know who you are. If you're not anyone important, there's no sense advertising it.

—*Modern Manners* (1983)

On my flight was a group of high-minded women—void of makeup, wearing earthy-hued clothing, and shod in enormous swarthy footwear. What is it about high-mindedness and big black shoes? If tootsies peek out the ends of little white Joan and David pumps, does this cause toenail painting? Does toenail painting lead to tanning parlors? After tanning parlors, what? These women could wind up at a Jimmy Buffett concert if they aren't careful.

—*Age and Guile Beat Youth, Innocence, and a Bad Haircut* (1995)

Maybe big black shoes are in the bylaws of People for the Ethical Treatment of Animals—so bugs can see your feet coming and avoid a horrible death by squashing.

—*Age and Guile Beat Youth, Innocence, and a Bad Haircut* (1995)

Chris Christie proved that the "portly man of fashion" has passed away. So long, Edward Prince of Wales, William Howard Taft, and Fats Domino. Maybe Christie's tough anti-immigrant stance scared off Omar the Tent-Maker. Christie had to get his suits from the guy who makes the tarps that cover boats in the driveways on the Jersey Shore.

—*How the Hell Did This Happen?* (2017)

Mark Zuckerberg in his Fruit of the Looms seems *too* comfortable. And this makes us mad.

There was a time when wealth was distributed far less equitably, but we weren't as resentful of the rich. We resented our poverty, but we were relieved that we didn't have to put on striped pants and spats to have breakfast.

—*A Cry from the Far Middle* (2020)

TEENAGERS

Teens are not taking nearly as many drugs as kids used to. This is not because they don't want to take drugs but there

are some drugs kids don't take today because their parents
took them all and there aren't any left.

—*Modern Manners* (1983)

When teenage dreams start coming true, sensible adults get
out of town.

—*Give War a Chance* (1992)

THE UNIVERSE

The universe, on close inspection, seems hardly to have been
an accident. Or, if it is an accident, it's certainly a complexly
ordered one—as if you dropped mushrooms, ham, truffles,
raw eggs, melted butter, and a hot skillet on the kitchen floor
and wound up with a perfect omelette.

—*Age and Guile Beat Youth, Innocence, and a Bad Haircut* (1995)

Frankly, scientific evidence cannot be ignored. And the scientific evidence instructs us conclusively that earth and its inhabitants enjoy that class of relationship to the cosmic whole which
we formerly reserved for red ants and two-headed brine shrimp.

—*Age and Guile Beat Youth, Innocence, and a Bad Haircut* (1995)

There are times you can abandon any attention to consequences, any inhibitions, any pretense to self-control and just
slide for weeks and still emerge unscathed. I don't know how
this works, and after you reach a certain age or position in
life it doesn't. It's like Saint Peter on the water, or a cartoon
character who has overrun a cliff—the instant you have a

self-conscious thought, you fall. But until then you slip away in an entropic blur of grace, immune to retribution for the havoc you generate. I often think the universe exists in this condition perpetually.

—*Age and Guile Beat Youth, Innocence, and a Bad Haircut* (1995)

VACATIONS

Like most people who don't own Bermuda shorts, I'm bored by ordinary travel.

—*Holidays in Hell* (1988)

The ideal Easter vacation for old guys is eight hours of sleep, a boss with the flu, and, in our wildest fantasy, a perky, buff, and willing young person who would reseed the lawn for less than $20 an hour.

—*The CEO of the Sofa* (2001)

WOMEN

On the subject of women I'm afraid there's nothing to say. And I, for one, don't want to be caught saying it.

—*Age and Guile Beat Youth, Innocence, and a Bad Haircut* (1995)

There are mysteries to female costume and body decoration that will never be plumbed by the human mind. Why, for instance, do women paint their lips, eyes, and the tips of their fingers and toes but not their noses, ears, or elbows?

—*Modern Manners* (1983)

Men are famously bad at translating the language of women's clothing. We often wrongly think an outfit is saying, "Come hither," when in fact it's saying, "This may be a Starbucks in Youngstown, Ohio, but there's always a *chance* that Channing Tatum will walk in. Go away."

　　　　　　　　　—How the Hell Did This Happen? (2017)

As near as I can tell, shopping is, for women, what hunting is for men. Except that they never get to use the remote control, battery-operated electric-shock dog collar on misbehaving store owners who are supposed to be helping them hunt for antiques. Also, as far as I'm concerned, a lot of antiques look like somebody's shot them already.

　　　　　　　　　—Holidays in Heck (2011)

WORRY

Constant money worries have a bad effect on human psychology. There is more unbalanced thinking about finance than about anything else. Death and sex may be the mainstays of psychoanalysis, but note that few shrinks ask to be paid in murders or marriages.

　　　　　　　　　—Eat the Rich (1998)

ZERO-SUM THINKING

If you get too many slices of pizza, I have to eat the Domino's box.

　　　　　　　　　—Don't Vote—It Just Encourages the Bastards (2010)

PART V

MEDIA AND MESSAGES

If the world is mad at America for anything, it should be for invention of the phone-in talk show.

—*Peace Kills* (2004)

The quality of what's communicated seems to decline steadily with every advance in the ease of communicating.

—*A Cry from the Far Middle* (2020)

ACCESS

The U.S. government, more than any other organization on earth, takes pains to provide journalists with "access" to make the lap-top La Rochefoucaulds feel that they are "present at the making of history." Of course, the same high honor can be had by going around to the back of any animal and "being present at the making of earth."

—Parliament of Whores (1991)

APPS

We'd like someone to develop an app that gets rid of all apps, a no-app app; call it a "napp."

—None of My Business (2018)

BOOK TOURS

By 11:00 A.M. the local TV audience has been driven to Nintendo and the unfortunate public relations firm employee has noticed that the author is showing dangerous quivering symptoms and needs to drink lunch soon. Lunch will be at a prestigious restaurant on a local newspaper reporter's lavish expense account. (You want that for here or to go?)

—Age and Guile Beat Youth, Innocence, and
a Bad Haircut (1995)

Most local newspaper editors consider the "book beat" to be somewhere in importance between scout meetings and Manitoba Provincial League curling scores.

—*Age and Guile Beat Youth, Innocence, and a Bad Haircut* (1995)

Reporters who are assigned to interview authors are either bad reporters who deserve no better than to interview authors or good reporters who have done something bad (usually to a bad reporter, e.g., releasing a box of live iguanas during her support group session) and are assigned to interview authors as punishment or they are young reporters who are assigned to interview authors because their editor doesn't know yet whether they are good enough to chase sensitive poetic types out of the newsroom with huge green lizards or bad enough to interview authors.

—*Age and Guile Beat Youth, Innocence, and a Bad Haircut* (1995)

Authors would like to go on "Trash TV" and throw chairs at Geraldo Rivera and Maury Povich and Morton Downey, Jr., but authors are never invited on these shows because most authors lead sedentary lives and can't throw a chair very far.

—*Age and Guile Beat Youth, Innocence, and a Bad Haircut* (1995)

CELEBRITIES

You can't shame or humiliate modern celebrities. What used to be called shame and humiliation is now called publicity.

—*Give War a Chance* (1992)

Is it just me or are there more celebrities nowadays than there are things to be celebrated?

—*The CEO of the Sofa* (2001)

Forget traditional character assassination. If you say a modern celebrity is an adulterer, a pervert and a drug addict, all it means is that you've read his autobiography.

—*Give War a Chance* (1992)

The New York Stock Exchange has achieved celebrity status. It appears on the network news every night and in the *New York Times* headlines every day, is kidded during talk show monologues, and attracts 700,000 tourists a year to live performances. Expect the secondary effects of fame to kick in soon. Nike merger-and-acquisition shoes. Tommy Hilfiger margin-call sweat suits.

—*Eat the Rich* (1998)

COMMUNICATION

Constant communication deprives us of an important part of communication—the part where we pause between communications and have time to accumulate experiences, knowledge, and thoughts that are worth communicating.

—*None of My Business* (2018)

COMPUTERS

I've never been fond of computers the way I'm fond of the stuff that *I* call hardware. Computers seem a little too adaptively flexible, like the strange natives, odd societies, and head cases we study in the social sciences.

—Holidays in Heck (2011)

My laptop may be a great technological improvement on my old IBM Selectric, but there is no historical indication that technological improvements in the way we inscribe our ideas lead to improvement in the wisdom, learning, and sense of the ideas themselves.

—A Cry from the Far Middle (2020)

CONTRARIANS

Just because people say the same thing over and over again doesn't mean it isn't true. There's no value in being contrarian just to be contrary.

—None of My Business (2018)

COSMOLOGIES

No wonder all the great intellectual concepts such as monotheism and using the zero in arithmetic come from pastoral societies where herdsmen sit around all night with nothing to do except think things up. (Though it *is* a wonder more cosmologies aren't founded on screwing sheep.)

—Parliament of Whores (1991)

CREATIVITY

I wonder how many people in the so-called creative fields stand before their accumulated professional efforts and think that the thing they've been doing for the past quarter of a century is a thing for which they have no particular talent. Not enough, to judge by the too copious output of various mature painters, poets, and architects. Hardly ever do we hear these people exclaim, "My pictures don't look like anything," "My poems don't rhyme," or "This isn't a building, it's the box a building comes in."

—*Age and Guile Beat Youth, Innocence, and a Bad Haircut* (1995)

CRYPTO

Crypto-currency adds a kind of unwelcome mysticism to the already baffling material and philosophical aspects of money. Some regard the blockchain with almost religious awe, as if it were the work of mythical "Geek Gods" high upon Mount Laptopus.

—*None of My Business* (2018)

Bitcoin seems like a weird scam invented by strange geeks with weaponized slide rules in the high school Evil Math Club.

—*None of My Business* (2018)

Crypto-currency on the World Wide Web does not create monetary security, or secrecy either. Money has always involved insecurities and secrets . . . [but] right now some dateless pear-shaped sixteen-year-old wearing emoji pajamas is in his bedroom with the floor covered in empty Snickers wrappers logging on to make himself a Darknet billionaire. I hope Walgreens accepts crypto-currency in payment for acne cream.

—None of My Business (2018)

DEBATE

More obnoxious than a joke is a heated debate. Not only is it aggressive, but it violates the spirit of conversation as an art form. A conversation is not expected to "decide something" any more than a painting by Matisse is.

—Republican Party Reptile (1987)

THE DIGITAL WORLD

There's more opposable thumb in the digital world than I care for; it's awfully close to human.

—Holidays in Heck (2011)

FAME AND FAMOUS PEOPLE

Fame is a communicable disease. And if you kiss the ass of someone who's got it, you may catch it yourself.

—Modern Manners (1983)

In order to meet famous people and give them the opportunity to take advantage of you, an introduction is necessary.

Asking for their autograph or running up to their restaurant table and gushing over their latest cause for notoriety ("I *loved* your divorce!") won't do.

—*Modern Manners* (1983)

Once you've met a famous person, say something that will make you remembered: "Cornelia Guest! Oh, my gosh, Miss Guest, I know it's polite for a gentleman to remove his hat when he meets a lady, but for you, I feel I should do something more, like take off my pants!!!" Then shut up. Famous people think they want to be treated like regular people. This is not true. Famous people also think they are special and wonderful. This is even less true. The best course of action is to go ahead and treat them as if they are ordinary (because, boy, are they ever) but now and then throw something into the conversation to show that you share their completely wrong-headed opinion of their own wonderfulness: "Gosh, Cornelia, you make liposuction *come alive!*"

—*Modern Manners* (1983)

FLATTERY

Flattery is like money.

—*Modern Manners* (1983)

GETTING ATTENTION

Get people to listen to you by keeping them involved in the conversation. Intersperse your comments about yourself with questions about them. Tell them how successful and clever you are, and then ask them who they sleep with and how much money they make. People so love attention that they may even tell you.

—Modern Manners (1983)

If you can't convince the world to love you, then scaring everyone out of their Bart Simpson Underachiever-and-Proud-of-It T-shirts is the next best way to get attention and feel needed.

—Give War a Chance (1992)

GOOGLE

Google is a very handy device for getting facts. If you don't mind the facts being wrong.

—None of My Business (2018)

GOSSIP

If you're like most people, you would prefer *not* to indulge in gossip and flattery. You would prefer to talk about yourself.

—Modern Manners (1983)

The problem is getting listeners. One way to do this is to disclose all your filthy habits, immoral actions, disgusting thoughts, and perverse longings.

—Modern Manners (1983)

If you're speaking to thieves, gossip about someone stealing. The thieves will have an intimate understanding of the subject and in addition will be flattered that you think they're honest: if you didn't, you wouldn't be talking about stealing in front of them.

—*Modern Manners* (1983)

Most sex acts take place in private and are easy to deny. Nothing indicts like a denial.

—*Modern Manners* (1983)

Whatever your piece of gossip is, be sure to tell your audience not to say you said it. This will remind them to say you did. It's an old trick and a sneaky one, but you don't want all the gruesome stories it took you so long to dig up being circulated without attribution.

—*Modern Manners* (1983)

HEADLINES

You'll never see a headline about how good things are. Especially not involving President Trump. His ability to grab the public's attention irks the news business, which thinks it should have a monopoly on grabbing the public. (Per Matt Lauer.) Thus, if Donald Trump cured cancer, the headlines would read, "Heart Disease Kills More People."

—*None of My Business* (2018)

HUMOR

There are several recognizable types of humorous activity. There is *parody*, when you make fun of people who are smarter than you; *satire*, when you make fun of people who are richer than you; and *burlesque*, when you make fun of both while taking off your clothes.

—*Age and Guile Beat Youth, Innocence, and a Bad Haircut* (1995)

The key to all types of humor probably lies in the folk saying "I didn't know whether to laugh or cry," or possibly in the folk saying "I didn't know whether to shit or go blind."

—*Age and Guile Beat Youth, Innocence, and a Bad Haircut* (1995)

Humor has nothing to do with the charming or the cheerful. Humor is how we cope with violated taboos and rising anxieties. Humor is our response to the void of absurdity. Humor comes to the fore when events render us impotent. And, as middle-aged men know, all events eventually do.

—*Age and Guile Beat Youth, Innocence, and a Bad Haircut* (1995)

Humor is not about a kitten tangled in a ball of yarn, unless—to steal a line from Michael O'Donoghue—the kitten strangles.

—*Age and Guile Beat Youth, Innocence, and a Bad Haircut* (1995)

The great advantage to humor as a trade is that ignorance has a positive value.

—*Age and Guile Beat Youth, Innocence, and a Bad Haircut* (1995)

People who worry themselves sick over sexism in language and think the government sneaks into their houses at night and puts atomic waste in the kitchen dispose-all cannot be expected to have a sense of humor. And they don't.

—Republican Party Reptile (1987)

IDEAS

Ideas may be distinguished from their duller cousins, opinions, in that ideas are living things which may be pruned, grafted onto, or forced to blossom as they pass around the table, whereas opinions are dead sticks most often used in thrashing equally dead equines.

—Republican Party Reptile (1987)

INFORMATION

Information is something everyone desires and no one has the patience to endure receiving.

—Republican Party Reptile (1987)

THE INTERNET

The New Economy is the Internet, which puts all the fools on earth in close personal touch.

—The CEO of the Sofa (2001)

The Internet began as a collaboration between the military and academia—two institutions that are good at spending money but which have never turned a profit. In fact, their missions are to be perfectly unprofitable, by breaking things and killing people in one case and turning young minds to mush in the other.

—*None of My Business* (2018)

I go back and forth on the virtues of the Internet. Sometimes I am awed by my instantaneous access to enormous troves of important information. "What was the name of the child actor who played Jerry Mathers' pudgy best friend Larry on *Leave It to Beaver?*" Other times I wonder, "Whose idea was it to put every idiot in the world in touch with every other idiot?" Larry was played by Rusty Stevens.

—*None of My Business* (2018)

INTERNET PRIVACY

The Internet treats user privacy with the same respect that snakes get in a cage at a carnival sideshow.

—*A Cry from the Far Middle* (2020)

JOKES

I became a foreign correspondent because I was tired of making bad jokes. I spent most of the Seventies as an editor at *The National Lampoon,* and I spent the early Eighties writing comedy scripts for movies and comic articles for magazines. All the while, the world outside seemed a much worse joke than anything I could conjure. "The secret source of humor itself is not joy but sorrow," said Mark Twain. I wanted to get at that awful source of mirth and make very, very bad jokes.

—Holidays in Hell (1988)

Radicals and liberals and such want all jokes to have a "meaning," to "make a point." But laughter is involuntary and points are not.

—Republican Party Reptile (1987)

JOURNALISM

A classical education provides no skills. Instead, I get to pursue that career of the professional amateur called journalism.

—Age and Guile Beat Youth, Innocence, and
a Bad Haircut (1995)

Anthropology is just travel writing about places that don't have room service, Sociology is journalism without news, and Psychology is peeking into your sister's diary after your parents have sent her to rehab.

—The CEO of the Sofa (2001)

The central idea of all automotive journalism: getting money to do what one would spend money to do if one hadn't found a way to be paid for doing it.

—Age and Guile Beat Youth, Innocence, and
a Bad Haircut (1995)

JOURNALISTS

I didn't mean to be a journalist. I meant to be a genius.
—*Age and Guile Beat Youth, Innocence, and a Bad Haircut* (1995)

Journalists aren't supposed to praise things. It's a violation of work rules almost as serious as buying drinks with our own money or absolving the CIA of something.
—*Give War a Chance* (1992)

Journalists are notoriously easy to kid. All you have to do is speak to a journalist in a very serious tone of voice, and he will be certain that you are either telling the truth or a big, important lie. It has never occurred to any journalist that he was having his leg pulled.
—*Parliament of Whores* (1991)

LAUGHTER

We laugh when we don't know what the fuck else to do.
—*Age and Guile Beat Youth, Innocence, and a Bad Haircut* (1995)

LISTEN UP

A drastic method of getting an audience: be one. Listen patiently while other people tell you about themselves. Maybe they'll return the favor. This is risky, however. By the time they get done talking about themselves and are ready to recipro-cate, you may be dead from old age. Another danger is that if you listen long enough you may start attending to what's being said. You may start thinking about other people, even sympathizing with them. You may develop a true empathy for others, and this will turn you into such a human oddity that you will become a social outcast.

—Modern Manners (1983)

LITERATURE

Unfortunately I didn't have the knack for literature. It seemed that a certain number of English professors had to have written brilliant, important, and deep Ph.D. dissertations on how no one would ever understand you. Also, it helped to be dead.

—Age and Guile Beat Youth, Innocence, and a Bad Haircut (1995)

LOGIN

In 1969 a UCLA student named Charley Kline tried to trans-mit the command "login" to a Stanford Research Institute computer on ARPANET. This caused the system to crash, and all that came through was "lo." About an hour later (if you think the people in Tech Support are bad now, imagine how bad they were when they didn't exist) the "gin" arrived. And I—shaken but not stirred—am still waiting for the olive and the vermouth.

—A Cry from the Far Middle (2020)

MAGAZINES

During the heyday of the glossy magazines the purpose of everything was *fun*—to provide the readers with some fun. And you can't give what you haven't got. The fun began Friday after work, at Brew's on Thirty-fourth Street in Manhattan around the corner from the *Car and Driver* offices. The fun adjourned to the bar at LaGuardia airport from which it was transported (with the aid of those libation-pouring stewardesses of yore) to David and Jeannie Davis's house in Ann Arbor, Michigan. And the fun, when last seen at about 3 A.M. Saturday morning, was drinking toasts out of the salad bowl and singing: "There once was a Spanish nobilio, Who lived in an ancient castillio. He was proud of his tra-la-la-lillio. And the works of his tweedle-dum dee."

—*Driving Like Crazy* (2009)

At the *National Lampoon* we parodied every type and style of prose. To do this it was necessary for us to understand the construction and workings of the objects of ridicule. My job was that of an aspiring watchmaker disassembling a fine timepiece. There I was with a thing of value and beauty, pulling it apart, ruining it for everyone, scattering small, useless springs and gears of irony and derision all over the literary workbench, and . . . Perhaps I should go back to the *National Lampoon* and study metaphor.

—*Age and Guile Beat Youth, Innocence, and a Bad Haircut* (1995)

We're cold-hearted conservatives here at the *American Spectator*. Heck, we have to call a Frigidaire service representative to get an EKG.

—*The Enemies List* (1996)

MAKING FUN

A conservative may tell you that you shouldn't make fun of something. "You shouldn't make fun of cripples," he may say. And he may be right. But a liberal will tell you, "You *can't* make fun of cripples." And he's wrong—as anybody who's heard the one about Helen Keller falling into a well and breaking three fingers calling for help can tell you.

—*Republican Party Reptile* (1987)

MEMOIR

Even though my memoir is still in the idea stage, I'm full of enthusiasm. I'll give the secret of my success—the success I plan to have as a memoir writer. As far as I can tell, the secret is thinking about myself all the time.

—*The CEO of the Sofa* (2001)

This isn't going to be a mere self-help book. This is the story of how one young man grew up to be . . . a lot older. The issue being that I haven't really done much. But I don't feel this should stand in my way. O.J. Simpson wrote a memoir, and the jury said he didn't do anything at all.

—*The CEO of the Sofa* (2001)

There's also a lot of anger I need to deal with. I'm angry at my parents. For memoir purposes, they weren't nearly poor enough.

—*The CEO of the Sofa* (2001)

As with all art, the memoir holds a mirror up to life, and if there are some lines of cocaine on that mirror, so much the better.

—The CEO of the Sofa (2001)

MONGOLIAN CLUSTER FUCK

"Mongolian Cluster Fuck" is the technical term journalists use for a preplanned, wholly scripted, news-free event. A summit conference is as interesting as a second cousin's wedding. Some stuff goes on that we might like a peek at, but it goes on behind locked doors. What we get to see is the bride and groom walking down the aisle.

—Holidays in Hell (1988)

MYSTICAL ENLIGHTENMENT

All our mystical enlightenments are now printed in Hallmark greeting cards. Our intellectual insights led to a school system that hasn't taught anybody how to read in fifteen years. All we've done for the disadvantaged is gentrify the crap out of their neighborhoods.

—Age and Guile Beat Youth, Innocence, and a Bad Haircut (1995)

OFF THE RECORD ON DEEP BACKGROUND

"I have to go take a Dukakis"—The phrase in quotations is a word-for-word off the record quote from Bush 41 obtained on deep background.

—How the Hell Did This Happen? (2017)

OPINIONS

Wouldn't it be great if we had an opinion-free news media source? I have the perfect name for it, "Happy Medium."

—*A Cry from the Far Middle* (2020)

OVEREXPOSURE

The worst punishment for dupes, pink-wieners, and dialectical immaterialists might be a kind of reverse blacklist. We don't prevent them from writing, speaking, performing, and otherwise being their usual nuisance selves. Instead, we hang on their every word, beg them to work, drag them onto all available TV and radio chat shows, and write hundreds of fawning newspaper and magazine articles about their wonderful swellness. In other words, we subject them to the monstrous, gross, and irreversible late-twentieth-century phenomenon of Media Overexposure so that a surfeited public rebels in disgust.

—*The Enemies List* (1996)

THE POWER OF THE WORD

"Weaponise" is my favorite new verb. The pen is mightier than the sword—until you weaponise your ballpoint to fight a man with a scimitar.

—*Peace Kills* (2004)

It's not just the written word that exhibits "degradation of the species."

> —*A Cry from the Far Middle* (2020)

PRINT

There are many compelling reasons to save America's print journalism. And I'll think of some while the bartender brings me another drink.

> —*Don't Vote—It Just Encourages the Bastards* (2010)

I once had hope that the fashion for recycling would rid me of my printed past. But what artisan—however modest his art— can bear to think that his life's work amounts to no more than the 1/100th part of the local Boy Scout paper drive?

> —*Age and Guile Beat Youth, Innocence, and a Bad Haircut* (1995)

PUBLIC IMAGE

Appearing in public on horseback does produce a more imposing effect than appearing in public on Twitter.

> —*None of My Business* (2018)

Mark Twain said, "Clothes make the man. Naked people have little or no influence on society." How wrong Twain was. "Naked and Afraid" might as well be the name of our era.

> —*How the Hell Did This Happen?* (2017)

PUBLIC RELATIONS

If a journalist shows a facility for praise he's liable to be offered a job in public relations or advertising and the next thing you know he's got a big office, a huge salary and is living in a fine home with a lovely wife and swell kids—another career blown to hell.

—*Give War a Chance* (1992)

PUBLIC TELEVISION

"AS SEEN ON PBS." Just four little words, yet oh how they catch the heart.

—*Parliament of Whores* (1991)

REPORTERS

If you spend seventy-two hours in a place you've never been, talking to people whose language you don't speak about social, political, and economic complexities you don't understand, and you come back as the world's biggest know-it-all, you're a reporter.

—*Holidays in Heck* (2011)

You say we [reporters] are distracting from the business of government. Well I hope so . . . Or maybe we should come over to your house and investigate *you*.

—*Age and Guile Beat Youth, Innocence, and a Bad Haircut* (1995)

Many reporters, when they go to work in the nation's capital, begin thinking of themselves as participants in the political process instead of as glorified stenographers.

—*Parliament of Whores* (1991)

The difference between journalists and other people is that other people spend their lives running from violence, tragedy, and horror and we spend ours trying to get in on it.

—*Republican Party Reptile* (1987)

Reporters who do duty in the third world spend a lot of time saying, "It's not that simple."

—*Republican Party Reptile* (1987)

RUMORS

I don't know exactly what happened, but I had a theory and I heard a rumor and the rumor I heard was close enough to the theory I had for the both of them to stand together in the place of fact.

—*Age and Guile Beat Youth, Innocence, and a Bad Haircut* (1995)

60 MINUTES

I'm not exactly sure why *60 Minutes* ended my commentator stint. My theory is that somebody at *60 Minutes* watched the show.

—*The CEO of the Sofa* (2001)

SMART OR STUPID

Whether smart is worse than stupid or vice versa is an important question. Smart people don't start many bar fights. But stupid people don't build many hydrogen bombs.

—*Republican Party Reptile* (1987)

SOCIAL MEDIA

Nobody's got *that* much to say.

—*A Cry from the Far Middle* (2020)

Social media should be drinking a big cup of shut up.

—*A Cry from the Far Middle* (2020)

Social media is giving young people a bad case of "phone face" with a big, permanent Samsung Galaxy Note 9 pimple between their eyes.

—*A Cry from the Far Middle* (2020)

Social media polarizes our politics by allowing us all—no matter how wrong we are about a political issue—to find a large, enthusiastic group of people who are even wronger.

—*A Cry from the Far Middle* (2020)

Social media is CB radio. "Breaker, breaker." "You copy?" "I'm wall to wall and treetop tall." "What's your handle, good buddy?" Except it lacks the intellectual depth. "And that's a big 10-4."

—*A Cry from the Far Middle* (2020)

With social media, we've done something worse than create a world where we can hear what everybody says. We've created a world where we can hear what everybody *thinks.*

—*A Cry from the Far Middle* (2020)

SOFTWARE

We have invented a brilliant matrix of complex and intricate software programs which allow us to compile, cross-reference, and instantly access all the nothing that we know.

—*Age and Guile Beat Youth, Innocence, and a Bad Haircut* (1995)

STATUS

Being unreachable is a potent status symbol in the world today.

—*The CEO of the Sofa* (2001)

STUPIDITY

Humans have a lock on stupid.

—*None of My Business* (2018)

You can get stupid results from computers—GIGO ("Garbage In/Garbage Out"). But it takes a human computer programmer to make it happen. Computers can think, but the smarter computers get the stupider they'll think stupidity is. And stupid makes the world go round. It's a big, stupid universe out there, with giant unwitting planets ignorantly spinning through moronic orbits around a thoughtless sun. And for what purpose? To what end? The very meaning of life is stupid. Ask yourself: What is the thing that demands stupidity, supplies stupidity, and has stupidity as its raw material and stupidity as its finished product?

—None of My Business (2018)

Stupidity is an excellent medium for vigorous conveyance of certain political ideas.

—The CEO of the Sofa (2001)

STUPID LOVE, STUPID JOB

The thing called love. A handsome visage, a pretty face—it's just an iris scan to a computer. But it's everything to us. We don't care how wonderfully stupid it makes us. Nor is our wonderful stupidity manifested only in romance. How could tottering toddlers, bumbling puppies, and kittens tangled in a ball of yarn make our hearts leap with joy if it weren't for stupidity—ours and theirs. How could we love all creation without a stupid grin on our face? Computers can't take our love away. And I don't believe computers can take our jobs away either. Consider your job for a moment. It's probably pretty stupid. That means a computer can't do it.

—None of My Business (2018)

TALKING

Why talk at all? How clever and original to be silent. No one does that.

—Modern Manners (1983)

TALK SHOWS

The business of trading embarrassment for money is an old American custom, dating back to the murky beginnings of the Phil Donahue show.

*—Age and Guile Beat Youth, Innocence, and
a Bad Haircut* (1995)

TELEVISED DEBATES

A nation that consumes as much booze and dope as we do and has our kind of divorce statistics should pipe down about "character issues." Either that or just go ahead and determine the presidency with three-legged races and pie-eating contests. It would make better TV.

—Parliament of Whores (1991)

So, why *did* I watch the Fox News/Facebook Republican Presidential Primary Debate? Why would *anyone* watch it? Unless he was drinking and had lost the channel changer? Which I was and did.

—How the Hell Did This Happen? (2017)

TELEVISION

Imagine the TV show *Cheers* set now. Theme song: "Where Everybody Knows Your Username." Sam and Diane, faces stuck in phones, never notice each other. Nobody yells "NORM!" or realizes that he's arrived. Waitress Carla isn't there, because drinks are ordered on menu touch screens. Woody delivers the drinks but doesn't have any funny hayseed lines. Cliff is still a know-it-all but he's posting everything he knows on his www.KnowItAll.com blog. And Frasier is busy providing virtual psychoanalysis.

—*None of My Business* (2018)

Our weapons are just TV shows and other such media pie fights that land with stupid splats like Sean Hannity and Rachel Maddow.

—*A Cry from the Far Middle* (2020)

TELEVISION NEWS

The idea of a news broadcast once was to find someone with information and broadcast it. The idea now is to find someone with ignorance and spread it around.

—*Give War a Chance* (1992)

TOOLS

I'm a sucker for anything that requires more equipment than I have sense.

—*Age and Guile Beat Youth, Innocence, and a Bad Haircut* (1995)

WAR REPORTING

You may wonder what the job of being a Gulf War journalist
is like. Well, we spend all day broadcasting on the radio and
TV telling people back home what's happening over here.
And we learn what's happening over here by spending all day
monitoring the radio and TV broadcasts from back home. You
may also wonder how any actual information ever gets into
this loop. If you find out, please call.

—Give War a Chance (1992)

WASHINGTON PRESS CORPS

If you can get accreditation to the Congressional Press Galleries—
which, when you're employed by a "major news outlet," is about
as difficult as falling asleep in a congressional hearing—you
receive a photo ID tag to wear on a chain around your neck.
Everybody who's anybody in Washington wears some kind of
ID tag on a chain around his neck, so that the place looks like
the City of Lost Dogs. I wore mine everywhere until one day in
the shower, when I had shampoo in my eyes, the chain caught
on the soap dish and I was nearly strangled by my own identity.
This happens a lot to members of the Washington press corps.

—Parliament of Whores (1991)

Washington journalists are seduced by their proximity to power.
Newsmen believe that news is a tacitly acknowledged fourth
branch of the federal system. This is why most news about government sounds as if it were federally mandated—serious, bulky
and blandly worthwhile, like a high-fiber diet set in type.

—Parliament of Whores (1991)

All of Washington conspires to make reporters feel important—a savvy thing to do to people who majored in journalism because the TV repair schools advertised on matchbook
covers were too hard to get into.

—Parliament of Whores (1991)

THE WEB

The web is just a device by which bad ideas travel around the
globe at the speed of light.

—The CEO of the Sofa (2001)

WORKING PRESS

I'm a member of the working press; you'd think I'd know
better than to listen to journalists.

—Give War a Chance (1992)

WRITERS

We writers live our whole lives on paper in the sincere hope
of never having to live them anywhere else.

—The CEO of the Sofa (2001)

Writers attract bores the way booze attracts writers.

—The CEO of the Sofa (2001)

I didn't even mean to be a writer. I meant to be a race-car driver, except I didn't have a race car. Or I meant to be a rock star, except I couldn't sing or play an instrument. (I know, I know, there are so many who haven't been stopped by that, but I was naive.)

—*Age and Guile Beat Youth, Innocence, and a Bad Haircut* (1995)

If wealth came from books I'd be too rich to be writing. I have no idea where power, success, and a big pile of money come from. Probably from someplace awful, such as hard work, or impossible, such as being much smarter than I am.

—*None of My Business* (2018)

WRITERS' TOOLS

The computer network is a handy device for writers. But does it improve the quality of what gets written? When words had to be carved in stone, we got the Ten Commandments. When we had to make our own ink and chase a goose around the yard to get a quill (and before the Infinite Monkey Theorem was developed), we got William Shakespeare. When the fountain pen was invented, we got Henry James. When the typewriter came along, we got Jack Kerouac. And with the Internet we get—the President of the United States on Twitter.

—*None of My Business* (2018)

WRITERS WORKSHOP

I came east to graduate school at Ivy Wannabe University where I was enrolled in its not very renowned Writers Workshop. This met twice a week and most of the class period was devoted, disappointingly, to the other workshop students reading aloud from their incomprehensible prose and poetry instead of me reading aloud from mine.

—*The Baby Boom* (2014)

WRITING

True life, even loudly exaggerated, has deficiencies in organization and plot line and a muddiness of symbolic content. It's hard to draw even the most common wisdom from the messy events of daily existence until they've been told over and polished and improved upon a few hundred times.

—*Age and Guile Beat Youth, Innocence, and a Bad Haircut* (1995)

One of the pleasures an author takes in writing acknowledgements is knowing that they go to press lightly edited.

—*Don't Vote—It Just Encourages the Bastards* (2010)

The difference between writing and the rest of the artistic endeavors used to be that the other artists had toys: saxophones, toe shoes, watercolors and oils. No writer ever sat down to work without feelings of bitter envy toward musicians, dancers, painters. Even the painters redoing the writer's apartment looked like they had it pretty good.

—*The CEO of the Sofa* (2001)

If what the author wrote was fiction, it's just something he made up. And, if what the author wrote was nonfiction, it's

just something he made up except for the names of celebrities.
This is what authors get for not listening to their mothers, who
said, "Always tell the truth, it's easier to remember."

—*Age and Guile Beat Youth, Innocence, and a Bad Haircut* (1995)

WRITING (PROCRASTINATION)

Usually, writers will do anything to avoid writing. For instance,
the previous sentence was written at one o'clock this afternoon. It is now a quarter to four. I have spent the past two
hours and forty-five minutes sorting my neckties by width,
looking up the word *paisley* in three dictionaries, attempting
to find the town of that name on *The New York Times Atlas of the
World* map of Scotland, sorting my reference books by width,
trying to get the bookcase to stop wobbling by stuffing a matchbook cover under its corner, dialing the telephone number on
the matchbook cover to see if I should take computer courses
at night, looking at the computer ads in the newspaper and
deciding to buy a computer because writing seems to be so
difficult on my old Remington, reading an interesting article
on sorghum farming in Uruguay that was in the newspaper next
to the computer ads, cutting that and other interesting articles
out of the newspaper, sorting—by width—all the interesting
articles I've cut out of newspapers recently, fastening them
neatly together with paper clips and making a very attractive
paper-clip necklace and bracelet set, which I will present to
my girlfriend as soon as she comes home from the three-hour
low-impact aerobic workout that I made her go to so I could
have some time alone to write.

—*Age and Guile Beat Youth, Innocence, and a Bad Haircut* (1995)

PART VI

MY GENERATION (BABY BOOMERS)

There are some things the Baby Boom has done that we're not proud of. We used up all the weird. It has always been the special prerogative of youth to look and act strange, to alarm and surprise their elders with peculiar dress and manners. But the Baby Boom exhausted the available supply of peculiar. Weird clothes, we wore them. Weird beards, we grew them. Weird words and phrases, we said them. Weird attitudes, we had them. Thus when it came time for the next generation to alarm and surprise us with their peculiarities, they were compelled to pierce their extremities and permanently ink their exposed flesh. Ouch. That must have hurt. We apologize.

—*The Baby Boom* (2014)

BABY BOOMERS

Those of us born between 1946 and 1964 constitute one third of the total U.S. population. And we're even worse than our parents. We're the most vapid, puling, screw-noodled, grabby and self-infatuated generation in history. Imagine what we'll be like—wearing roller skates with our walkers, buying Ralph Lauren cashmere colostomy bags, going to see Jackson Browne impersonators at Atlantic City and grumbling that our heart-lung machines have gone condo. Woe to any youngster in the year 2030 who happens to get cornered by one of us when we start reminiscing about the sixties. "Bring the stun ray quick, Ma, Granddad's going into a Nixon fit again!!!"

—*Parliament of Whores* (1991)

BEHOLD THE BABY BOOM

When we really are the world the place will be chaos. A universal Baby Boom will be running around everywhere doing anything they want at all hours of the day and night with nobody left to clean up. It may be a bad world. But it will be a worse world for the Leaders of Men, looking around for their followers and wondering why everyone is following Keith Richards. It will be a terrible world for Authority. The Baby Boom will not countenance it. We turn our face from Authority. Indeed we turn our ass toward it. We moon Dominion.

Woe to you who have oppressed mankind with your theologies and your ideologies, your bigotries, doctrines, dogmas, and no sex until after we're married. Desolation awaits you who have foisted war upon us, subjugated us, yoked us, fettered us, and told us we can't get down and boogie.

You shall be as the ants beneath our magnifying glasses, the sand wasps affronted with our tennis rackets, the frogs ingesting our fireworks, the cats between our garages, the birdbaths, garden gnomes, and glass gazing balls at the mercy of our Wham-O slingshots. Flaming bags of dog poop shall be set upon your front porches.

Think how we made a misery of the lives of our parents. If we can do that to our dearest beloved, think what we can do to you. For that matter think what we did to ourselves. You shall spend eternity at a "Model UN." You shall listen forever to lectures of Margaret Mead. You shall sit upon a staircase inside a giant evil eel for all time. And if you go upstairs you'll be chewed by giant eel teeth. And if you go downstairs you'll be eel shit.

We are an obdurate generation. Our whim is iron. What we will to do is done. You, eel shit members of the Chinese politburo, have had a taste of this in Tiananmen Square. You remember the fellow blocking the tank. But do you remember the crucial detail? He was carrying shopping bags. Not only were you violating his human liberties, you were interfering with his shopping, a Baby Boom birthright. One man is a majority with shopping on his side.

You loathsome communists got away with it in Tiananmen Square. But for how long? The vengeance of the Baby Boom can be delayed but not denied. There will come a day, Xi Jinping, when the power and the dignity of your office shall be rendered so low that you shall appear as guest host on *Saturday Night Live*.

And what about you, detestable Taliban and Al-Qaeda and Osama wannabes cowering in your Waziristan, Kandahar, Yemen, and Mali hidey-holes? You who are pursued by those things perfectly christened with the name Baby Boomers have so often been called, drones. And when it comes to Baby Boom lethal technology, drones are nothing. How will things be with you when your bevy of wives discover vibrators? And you, contemptible Putin? How long will your shirtless self escape the LGBT float in the Greenwich Village Halloween Parade?

And all the rest of you tyrannical, despotic, overbearing squares and wet smacks with your two-bit autocracies in the butt ends of the world? You shall gather in finished basements while your revered elders stand at the top of the basement stairs yelling, "I think something's on fire down there!" Your offices shall be liberated by Balto-Cong. You shall spend your treasure on cocaine and rehab. Your junk bonds shall default. You shall form overage garage bands and try to play "Margaritaville." Your third spouse shall acquire an American Express Black Card with a credit limit higher than the U.S. national debt. Your daughters shall wear nose rings. Your sons shall have pagan symbols indelibly marked upon their necks. (Unless you belong to one of those cultures where daughters wear nose rings and sons have pagan symbols indelibly marked upon their necks, in which case they shall not.) You shall be perplexed by the Internet. You shall grow old and addled enough to vote for Ron Paul in a presidential primary.

There is no escape from happiness, attention, affection, freedom, irresponsibility, money, peace, opportunity, and finding out that everything you were ever told is bullshit. Behold the Baby Boom, ye mighty, and despair.

—*The Baby Boom* (2014)

BLAME

Either we blame it on drugs or we blame it on ourselves. And let's not be silly.

—*The Baby Boom* (2014)

BOARD GAMES

Board games and card games were for rainy days, and if it looked like the rain was never going to stop we'd get out Monopoly. Despairing of its page upon page of rules we'd make our own. This is how both Wall Street investment strategy and Washington economic policy were invented by our generation.

—*The Baby Boom* (2014)

BOY SCOUTS

Scouting was Sunday school with mission creep. There was God *and* Country and for some reason both were in the Great Outdoors. The proper way to show respect for God and Country when They were outdoors was to adopt pseudo-military dress and behavior.

—*The Baby Boom* (2014)

Most Scouting was done in the church gymnasium, but at least it was on a weeknight. I remember maybe three camping trips in my five years of desultory participation in the Boy Scouts. It rained.

—*The Baby Boom* (2014)

CHILDHOOD

For a few blissful years, between the time the *Enola Gay* landed and the time the helicopter parents took off, children were in control of childhood. There were some rules. Everybody outdoors on nice days, no crossing busy streets, no hitting girls, no firecrackers in your mouth, come when you're called for dinner, and everybody indoors when the streetlights go on. These rules, like the definition of a "nice day," were broadly construed. They were enforced by the general committee of grown-ups with the inefficiency for which committees are famous. All eyes were upon us in the neighborhood but not looking too closely. And so we ran wild—in a rather tame manner.

—The Baby Boom (2014)

We seldom knocked on doors and never, except on Halloween, rang doorbells. When we wanted to contact a friend, the accepted form was to stand outside his house and shout his name at the top of our lungs, "Oh, Bill*eeey!*," with the last syllable greatly prolonged and shrilly emphasized. "Oh, Bill*eeey!*" could be heard a block and a half away. If a kid lived more than a block and a half away, we didn't know him.

—The Baby Boom (2014)

COMING-OF-AGE

When we came of age in the 1960s, we found the world wasn't as perfect as Mr. Green Jeans and Ozzie Nelson said it would be, and we threw a decade-long temper tantrum. We screamed at our parents, our teachers, the police, the president, Congress, and the Pentagon. We threatened to hold our breath (as long as the reefer stayed lit) and not cut our hair until poverty, war, and injustice were stopped. That didn't work. So we whiled away the 1970s in an orgy of hedonism and self-absorption, bouncing from ashram to bedroom to disco to gym at a speed made possible only by ingesting vast quantities of Inca Scratch N Sniff.

—Age and Guile Beat Youth, Innocence, and a Bad Haircut (1995)

CONFUSION

I was confused about the connection between actions and consequences in general. Or I was once most of the coeds had prescriptions for the pill.

—The Baby Boom (2014)

COONSKIN CAPS

We're a pathetic bunch. And it didn't start with the Beatles, marijuana, and the pill. Recall the coonskin cap. I wore mine to school. Children of previous eras may have worn coonskin caps but they had to eat the raccoons first.

—Don't Vote—It Just Encourages the Bastards (2010)

DAMAGE

Emptying government coffers is the least of the damage that we baby boomers intend to inflict over the next thirty or forty years. What we're really up to is something more diabolical. Our generation is going to do what our generation has always done best. We're going to shape the American social fabric to our will and make the entire nation conform to our ideals, judgments, and tastes.

—Don't Vote—It Just Encourages the Bastards (2010)

DRUGS

From about 1967 until John Belushi died we created a way of life based almost entirely on drugs. And we can do it again.

—*Don't Vote—It Just Encourages the Bastards* (2010)

FADS

It is claimed that the Baby Boom youth was a period of great faddishness due to the growing powers of savvy on Madison Avenue and television mass marketing—coonskin caps, Frisbees, hula hoops, Pez dispensers. And this faddishness, in turn, is claimed to signify something about the Baby Boom. Perhaps. Faddishness seems a constant in human affairs—phone booth stuffing, "Killroy Was Here," flagpole sitting, muttonchop sideburns. The fad for dying of tuberculosis may have signified something about the Victorian Age. Ascribe significance to the hula hoop, you who can.

—*The Baby Boom* (2014)

FEELINGS

A generational truth was discovered. How people feel about things is as important as things. Feelings are real. And now so were girls. You could feel them. Eventually. But you had to talk to them about feelings first. (For girls, boys got real too—until talking to us about feelings got unreal at the end of the first marriage.)

—*The Baby Boom* (2014)

THE FRESHMEN AMONG US

They're still Baby Boomers. The freshmen may be different in many ways from the Baby Boom's upper classmen, but there's no mistaking them for members of any of the younger and duller (if hotter) generations. The tip-off is the blather, the jabber, the prattle, the natter, the gab, gas, yak, yap, baloney, blarney, bunkum, the jaw-slinging, tongue-wagging, gum-beating chin music that is the Baby Boom's gift to the world. Stephen Colbert is a freshman. So is Ann Coulter. So are Jon Stewart, Sarah Palin, Conan O'Brien, and Larry the Cable Guy.

—The Baby Boom (2014)

To freshmen the Vietnam War was just something that was inexplicably on TV all the time, like Ed McMahon. Feminism had gone from a pressing social issue to a Bea Arthur comedy show that their parents liked, and, by the time the freshmen were in college, feminism was an essay topic for the "Reading Shakespeare in Cultural Context" course. Hint: Lady Macbeth hit that glass ceiling hard.

—The Baby Boom (2014)

Freshmen have no personal memory of the Kennedy and King assassinations, which showed the tragedy inherent in greatness and taught the Baby Boom to stop just short of it, the way Bill Clinton did. They may have suffered a momentary golden oldies pang when John Lennon was shot, thinking, maybe, "Now the original Wings will never be reunited."

—The Baby Boom (2014)

THE GENERATION GAP

A great clash between youth and age began. A generation gap yawned. And so do I. It never happened. We had parents who were a lot like us. We can tell because they've shown up in the mirror.

—The Baby Boom (2014)

THE GREATEST GENERATION

The Greatest Generation integrated the armed forces and Little Rock Central High, passed the Civil Rights Act, sent their daughters to law school, and founded the gay liberation movement by watching Liberace on TV. Our gripe with them is that they did the right thing without being enthusiastic about it. Why couldn't they be more like the Baby Boom is with recycling and proudly celebrate time spent in the trash bin of human behavior separating vice from virtue?

—The Baby Boom (2014)

My glowing toddler memory is Dad coming home from work. The Greatest Generation arrives. The sight of my father driving up the driveway produces an exultant thrill. And not just because he often brought a toy.

—The Baby Boom (2014)

During the 1960s we would talk about our parents, as a group, in a way that today we would be embarrassed to talk about militant Islamic fundamentalists, as a group. Our depth and breadth of prejudice would shock every one of our twenty-first-century sensibilities, if we ever thought about it. Which we don't because, later still, we got all soppy and sentimental about the Greatest Generation just in time to put them in nursing homes or the grave.

—*The Baby Boom* (2014)

GROWING UP

The Baby Boom faced a difficulty in leaving childhood behind. We had no motive to do so.

—*The Baby Boom* (2014)

HAVING IT ALL

We elected President Reagan and tried our hand at naked greed. We could have it all—career, marriage, job, children, BMW, Rolex, compact disc player, another marriage, more children, and a high-growth, high-yield, no-load mutual fund. Actually, for a while, it looked like we *could* have it all. As long as we didn't mind also having a national debt the size of the Crab Nebula, an enormous underclass making its living from five-cent beverage can deposits, and currency that the Japanese use to blow their noses. But now our economy has the williwaws, and our Youth Culture has arthritis, Alzheimer's, and gout. Life's big Visa card bill has come due at last.

—*Age and Guile Beat Youth, Innocence, and a Bad Haircut* (1995)

HIGHER EDUCATION

I belonged to that great tradition of academic bohemia which stretches from the fifteenth- century riots of François Villon's to the Phish tours of the present day. For university hipsters, there is (no doubt Villon mentions this in his Petit Testament) nothing more pathetic than taking business courses. My friends and I were above that. In our classes we studied literature, anthropology, and how to make ceramics. We were seeking, questing, growing. Specifically, we were growing sideburns and leg hair, according to gender. It did not occur to us that the frat-pack dolts and Tri-Delt tweeties, hurrying to get to Econ 101 on time (in their square fashion), were the real intellectuals.

—*Eat the Rich* (1998)

"THE HIGH SIXTIES"

It was a decade without quality control. And it was not, of course, a decade. The "sixties," as they are popularly remembered— what might too well be called "The High Sixties"—was an episode of about seventy-two months' duration that started in 1967 when the Baby Boom had fully infested academia and America's various little bohemian enclaves such as Greenwich Village, Haight-Ashbury, Big Sur, and the finished basement at my house and came to an abrupt halt in 1973 when conscription ended and herpes began.

—*The Baby Boom* (2014)

HIPPIES

I *liked* being a hippie pretend guerrilla writing horrible long poems to Suzy and Moonbeam and Babs. I had a great time thinking I could end war and social injustice by letting my hair grow and dressing like a circus clown. And—though we're not supposed to say it these days—the drugs were swell.

—*Age and Guile Beat Youth, Innocence, and a Bad Haircut* (1995)

LONGEVITY

Those of us who were born when postwar birthrates were highest, even before Ike was liked, won't (statistics tell us) have to wait as long for death as we had to wait to get laid. We'd be sad about this if we weren't too busy remarrying younger wives, reviving careers that hit glass ceilings when children arrived, and renewing prescriptions for drugs that keep us from being sad.

—*The Baby Boom* (2014)

METAMORPHOSIS

We made the universe personal, and we made the universe new. New in the sense of juvenescent. We have an abiding admiration for our own larval state. We saw that the grown-ups were like primitive insects. They never underwent metamorphosis. They didn't emerge from their home and office cocoons with brilliant, fluttering wings. They just continued to molt, getting more gross, lumpy, and

bald and, as it were, bugging us. Better that we should stay
nymphs and naiads. Plus we were having more fun than the
adults of the species.

—The Baby Boom (2014)

MOM AND DAD

Our fathers weren't household tyrants. They weren't even
home that often. . . . And our moms were "understanding." They'd read Dr. Spock, women's magazines, and
newspaper advice columnists. Maybe they couldn't bring
themselves to discuss sex in detail but, in general, you
couldn't shut them up about "the changes young people
are going through."

—The Baby Boom (2014)

I remember riding in the car with my mother, lolling around
on the front seat as children were allowed to do. I looked at
her face, sunlit in profile, and was so stricken by her beauty
and so overwhelmed by my love for her that I reached over
and pulled the hood release on the Buick.

—The Baby Boom (2014)

NEIGHBORS

Our neighbors came from farm villages, small towns, row
houses, and tenements, all of which were snug and ethnic
even when the ethnicity was an unspiced American mix of

English, German, and Scots-Irish. Everybody was some kind of shirttail cousin or a friend of the family from way back or had jilted your dad's sister. The old neighborhoods were close-knit in an itchy, scratchy way. When everyone moved out it was a relief to all concerned.

—The Baby Boom (2014)

NEW NEIGHBORHOODS

In the new neighborhoods you didn't know the other people very well so you had the luxury of pretending to like them. Great store was put on neighborliness, meaning that you took a casserole next door if a neighbor had received a phone call after 9 P.M. And sometimes you dropped over unannounced, with children. People did indeed sit on the front porch and wave to other people sitting on other front porches. And they dutifully continued to do so until the minute a screened-in back porch was added to their house.

—The Baby Boom (2014)

THE NOW GENERATION

Look at the hip young men walking around in their high-water pants, wearing stupid bowling shirts buttoned up to the collar. A bunch of twenty-six-year-olds are going to coffee shops (coffee shops! how *antique!*) dressed as their grandpas.

—Don't Vote—It Just Encourages the Bastards (2010)

NUCLEAR HOLOCAUST

And every couple of months we'd have a real air-raid drill and get under our desks to protect ourselves from nuclear holocaust. But we knew that atomic bombs only killed grownups and probably caused school to be let out early. Billy and I and Johnny and Steve and Bobby and Jerry would survive, like in *Lord of the Flies* but without the flies. Not that I'd read the book, or heard of it. But when I did read it I was impressed anew with the capacity of adults like William Golding to spoil things.

—*The Baby Boom* (2014)

PARENTS AND PARENTING

We had parents. They brought us up. We are what our parents, consciously or unconsciously, meant us to be. We're the demiurge to their urgency. They were the thought to our deed. It's an irritating supposition.

—*The Baby Boom* (2014)

We in the Baby Boom had an unadulterated love for our parents that few children, past or future, have matched. Maybe we surpassed what other children felt for their parents because, in the past, children grew up in colder and more crowded homes with mushier meals and the razor strap still hanging by the bathroom sink, and, in the future, children had us for moms and dads.

—*The Baby Boom* (2014)

Our parents picked a particular house by making a complex calculation based on the likelihood of children getting run over on busy streets factored into the walking distance to the local grade school. (Incidentally, what old-fashioned parents thought of as walking distance to school was much longer than it is now, almost as long as what modern parents think of as a healthy morning run.) Then they checked to make sure the basement was dry. Wet basements gave children a cough. You could show our parents Buckingham Palace and all they'd say is "It's on a busy street" and "Does it have a dry basement?"

                                       —*The Baby Boom* (2014)

Our parents didn't get divorced. They didn't hit us much. If they were neurotic they had the good manners to have a drink instead of a long talk with us about it. They were stricter than we would be with our kids. But they were less pestering and intrusive. A Greatest Generation parent was as likely to turn up at school blaming a teacher for his kid's poor arithmetic grade as Xi Jinping is likely to turn up at Amnesty International blaming Bono for his country's poor human rights record. Our parents may have been distant by modern standards, but a certain distance is helpful in adulation.

                                       —*The Baby Boom* (2014)

PETER PAN

We weren't the first generation to fly around the room under the influence of pixie dust, act like fools with girls who called themselves "Tinker Bell" and "Tiger Lily," battle an imagined villain such as Hook—be he captain of pirate ship, industry, police force, or army—and string Wendy along for years while she yearned for a home and children of her own. But we were the generation that did it best.

—*The Baby Boom* (2014)

THE PIONEERS

We studied the handicrafts, songs, and square dances of the American pioneers. We knew everything about frontier life except when it happened and why.

—*The Baby Boom* (2014)

POWER

Baby Boomers are not power hungry. Power comes with that kicker, responsibility. We're greedy for love, happiness, experience, sensation, thrills, praise, fame, adulation, inner peace, and, as it turns out, money. Health and fitness too. But we're not greedy for power. Observe the Baby Boomers who have climbed to its ascendency in Washington. The best and the brightest? They're over at Goldman Sachs.

—*The Baby Boom* (2014)

PRETENDING

Pretending had a lot to do with neighborliness. The neighborhoods of the 1950s were as make-believe as the Walt Disney Company's planned community, Celebration. But there was as yet no such job description as "imagineering." Our parents had to pretend without professional assistance, in their own unimaginative ways.

—*The Baby Boom* (2014)

Pretend the entire world is our school and all the prominent people are students in my class. What's everybody up to? The popular kids are out having fun. The smart kids are reading Adam Smith. The ambitious kids are working nights and weekends. The talented kids are playing sports and rehearsing for the school play. I'm drinking beer behind the Dairy Queen. And the insufferable twits? They're running for student government.

—*The CEO of the Sofa* (2001)

PROBLEMS

We number more than 75 million, and we're not only diverse but take a thorny pride in our every deviation from the norm (even though we're in therapy for it). We are all alike about us each being unusual. Fortunately we are all alike about big, broad problems too. We won't face them.

—*The Baby Boom* (2014)

Triathlon (was) a Baby Boom innovation of the middle 1970s. By then we knew we couldn't run away from our problems. *But* if we added cycling and swimming . . .

—*The Baby Boom* (2014)

PUNK

By the end of the 1970s the Baby Boom character had been formed. Our last youthful exuberance, "Punk," came just before Generation X's first youthful exuberance, "Goth"—a subtle shift from "fuck you" to "I'm fucked" that indicates the Baby Boom will remain in control for a long time to come.

—*The Baby Boom* (2014)

RETIREMENT

We'll never retire. We can't. The mortgage is underwater. We're in debt up to the Rogaine for the kids' college education. And it serves us right—we're the generation who insisted that a passion for living should replace working for one.

—*The Baby Boom* (2014)

THE ROAD NOT TAKEN

Although Robert Frost had an effect on the 1960s. "The Road Not Taken." *I took the one less traveled by, and that has made all the difference.* Then everybody took the road less traveled by, and that made the 1960s.

—*The Baby Boom* (2014)

SAINTS

Saints were all over the place with special powers like comic book superheroes but more numerous and more outlandishly

costumed although beset with really a lot of Kryptonite causing them to be martyred all the time.

—The Baby Boom (2014)

SCHOOL

School started at 8:30. Before the doors opened, children
were expected to form two lines, one for the boys and one for
the girls. The boys pushed each other. The girls teased each
other. We would have been better behaved if we'd been mixed
together, but the people who insist on organizing life and the
people who have no idea how life is organized were and always
will be the same people.

—The Baby Boom (2014)

SELF

We are the generation that changed everything. Of all the
eras and epochs of Americans, ours is the one that made the
biggest impression—on ourselves.

—The Baby Boom (2014)

We're the generation that created the self, made the firma-
ment of the self, divided the light of the self from the darkness
of the self, and said let there be self. If you were born between
1946 and 1964, you may have noticed this *your*self.

—The Baby Boom (2014)

SEX

My life would have gone along perfectly well, politically speaking, if it hadn't been for girls. I found them interesting. They found me less so.

—*Don't Vote—It Just Encourages the Bastards* (2010)

We got over it, the same way we got over sexual liberation when we found out that the viruses were having all the reproductive fun.

—*The CEO of the Sofa*, p. 85

SOCIAL SECURITY

How can current Social Security allotments be expected to fund our skydiving, bungee jumping, hang gliding, and whitewater rafting, our skiing, golf, and scuba excursions, our photo safaris to Africa, bike tours of Tuscany, and sojourns at Indian ashrams, our tennis clinics, spa treatments, gym memberships, personal fitness training, and cosmetic surgery, our luxury cruises to the Galápagos and Antarctica, the vacation homes in Hilton Head and Vail, the lap pools, Jacuzzis, and clay courts being built thereat and the his and hers Harley-Davidsons?

And we haven't even touched on the subject of Social Security's civil union life partner, Medicare. It won't take much skydiving, bungee jumping, hang gliding, and whitewater rafting before we all require new hips, knees, and elbows, fused spinal discs, pacemakers, and steel plates in our heads. The expense of these will be as nothing compared to the cost of our pharmacological needs. Remember, we are the generation that *knows* drugs.

—*Don't Vote—It Just Encourages the Bastards* (2010)

SOFT

We weren't soft kids. We aren't a soft generation. We couldn't be or we wouldn't keep getting our own way. And we've been doing so for more than sixty years.

—*The Baby Boom* (2014)

Our parents called us soft because we didn't get up at 4 A.M. to help Pa drag a mop through the dust bowl or wear underpants made of barrel staves because Ma couldn't afford burlap or work two jobs to put ourselves through grade school or squat in the basement all night with a piece of cheese in our hand because mousetraps were too expensive.

—*The Baby Boom* (2014)

We kids were called soft because we didn't go through what our parents went through, which they were usually lying about. And now *we* call kids soft—their flabby fingers plopping out text messages, bodies barely capable of enough wiggle for Wii, mounds of suet parked in front of LED screens with body mass indexes to make Jerry Harris look like Olga Korbut. I say that and then I go outside and see kids on skateboards and funny little bicycles and snowboards and twin-tip skis doing things that would have scared the worst word I knew out of me in 1959.

—*The Baby Boom* (2014)

SPORTS

Our parents didn't come down from the stands at our games and hit coaches, opposing players, and each other in swell melees that went viral and got, like, a million hits on You-Tube. Such behavior was inconceivable. It would have meant that our parents had come to our games. Our parents were home getting a little peace and quiet while sports "kept us out of trouble."

—*The Baby Boom* (2014)

SPORTSMANSHIP

We suffered from an emphasis on good sportsmanship. We weren't allowed to pump our fists in the air, exchange high fives, do sack dances, or prance around in the end zone as if we had Deep Heat in our jockstraps. We were reduced to bragging to smaller children out of adult earshot.

—*The Baby Boom* (2014)

THE SUBURBS

Teenage 1960s middle-class America was a shining suburb on a hill. Almost twenty years would go by before we realized that. We've been trying to walk or fly or bum a ride back there since the first John Hughes movie came out.

—*The Baby Boom* (2014)

SUPPORT GROUPS

There's a website for that, a support group to join, a class to take, alternative medicine, regular exercise, a book that explains it all, a celebrity on TV who's been through the same thing, or we can eliminate gluten from our diet. History is full of generations that had too many problems. We are the first generation to have too many answers.

—*The Baby Boom* (2014)

TEACHERS

The teacher was, until junior high, invariably a woman, usually single, and alone at her station of command. Teachers' aides had not yet been sent to the aid of teachers. Busybody parents weren't sticking their noses in from the back row. Elected representatives of the school board weren't visiting to make sure that the curriculum was conformist, or that the curriculum was nonconformist, according to which kind of nut won the school board election. Not that our teachers needed such assistance. They wielded the kind of unalloyed power that God used to have in the Old Testament before 1950s Sunday school teachers got to Him.

—*The Baby Boom* (2014)

TEAMWORK

The Greatest Generation was big on teamwork. I can't think why. They'd just lost China with their Chiang Kai-shek team, been stalemated in Korea on the UN team, and were in the middle of a Cold War that was the result of having been former teammates with the Soviet Union.

—*The Baby Boom* (2014)

When corporations teamed up it was called a monopoly and needed to be stopped with antitrust laws. When workers teamed up it was called Jimmy Hoffa and needed to be investigated by the FBI. But out on the sports field we were told, "There is no 'I' in team." And what with the way we were taught to spell in the 1950s, we had to think about that one.

—The Baby Boom (2014)

TELEPHONES

Children were forbidden independent use of the telephone. Any other form of personal communication technology, had it existed, would have been considered ridiculous. Adults themselves didn't use the telephone any more than necessary. Party lines were still common. Two rings for the Andersons, one ring for us. To say something on a party line was to tell the world. That it would be wonderful to tell the world one's every thought and feeling hadn't occurred to people yet.

—The Baby Boom (2014)

Our house had a single phone, in the dining room on a shelf in a nook specifically designed to accommodate it. A call after 9 P.M. meant, at best, that someone in the family had died. Either that or the call had been prearranged, by mail, with my mother's sister in Chicago, to take advantage of lower nighttime long-distance rates. On long-distance calls Grandma shouted. It was, after all, a long distance.

—The Baby Boom (2014)

TROUBLED ADOLESCENTS

Perhaps there were as many troubled adolescents then as there are now. But being troubled wasn't in style. Girls weighed ninety pounds and barfed after eating a whole half gallon of butter pecan ice cream. Boys drove cars into phone poles at seventy miles an hour. But anorexia, bulimia, and teenage suicide were unheard of.

—The Baby Boom (2014)

VANDALISM

I was, I confess, never really very good at rioting. I weighed only about 130 pounds in those days, so any liberties I trampled were trampled upon lightly. I was too fundamentally middle class to be much of a vandal. I was pretty sure that if I smashed a store window my mother would pop up out of nowhere, snap a dish towel at me, and yell, "Windows don't grow on trees! They cost money! Somebody worked hard to make the money for that window! And it's coming out of *your* allowance!"

—None of My Business (2018)

VENGEANCE

We baby boomers are growing old, but growing old with a vengeance. Our hands may be palsied and arthritic but we hold America's fate in them. And America's fate can be summed up in one word: *youthanasia.*

—Don't Vote—It Just Encourages the Bastards (2010)

WE ARE THE PEOPLE . . .

A supposition the Baby Boom prefers is that we're mutants. "We are the people our parents warned us about." The Jimmy Buffett song was released in 1983, by which time we were indeed the people our parents had warned us about—lawyers, bankers, and politicians.

—The Baby Boom (2014)

WEATHERPEOPLE

Weathermen leaders Bernardine Dohrn and Bill Ayers never were captured. They had to turn themselves in, in 1980. Now they're passing acquaintances of the president of the United States. Some say this is dim of the president. Some say this is hypocritical of Bernardine and Bill. But, in the far reaches of our hearts, we, with our deep Baby Boom dislike of the consequential, say, "Is this a great country or what?"

—The Baby Boom (2014)

WHAT WENT WRONG?

We were the generation of hope; the generation that was going to change the world; the biggest, richest, best-educated generation in the history of America—the biggest, richest, best-educated spot in this or any other galaxy. Nothing was too good for us. It took thousands of doctors and psychiatrists to decide whether we should suck our thumbs or all our toes, too. Our every childhood fad had global implications. One smile at Davy Crockett and the forests of the temperate zone were leveled in the search for raccoon-tail hats. When we took up hula hoops, the planet bobbled in its orbit. Our transistor radios drowned out the music of the spheres. A sniffle from us and *Life* magazine was sick in bed for a month. All we had to do was hold a sit-in and governments were toppled from the Beijing of Mao Tse-tung to the Cleveland of Dennis Kucinich. "We are the world," we shouted just a couple of years ago. And just a couple of years ago we were. How did we wind up so old? So fat? So confused? So *broke?*

—*Age and Guile Beat Youth, Innocence, and a Bad Haircut* (1995)

YEARBOOKS

"Don't ever change!" we wrote in each other's high school yearbooks. "Stay just the way you are!" What strange valedictions to give ourselves on the threshold of life. Imagine if we had obeyed them, and now everyone possessed the resolute solipsism of adolescence with its wild enthusiasms, dark lethargies, strong lusts, keen aversions, inner turmoils, and uncontained impulses. Life would be exactly like it is today. You're welcome.

—*The Baby Boom* (2014)

ACKNOWLEDGMENTS

Special thanks to Sara Vitale, who led the original gathering of material from all of P. J. O'Rourke's books.

Thank you to Charley Burlock, who wrangled a second wave and conducted specific searches.

Thanks also go to the following research contributors: Dylan Croll, George Gibson, Elliot Kaufman, Alice Lloyd, Hannah Long, Windsor Mann, and Andrew Unger.